What people are saying abo

"So many people fail to recover because they don't know where to start when they stop. David tells you where to start and guides you along the path in this wonderful Twelve Step book. Read it, because it could make all the difference in the world."
STEVE ARTERBURN, Author & Founder of Women of Faith; Host of NewLife "Live"

"You will find *Our Journey Home* to be a remarkable new friend in your journey towards wholeness and integrity. As you read this book, you will meet the heart of David Zailer through the stories he tells, and the scriptural insights he offers without a hint of judgment or shame. You will find yourself moving from the destructive paths of addiction to the refreshing freedom found in grace, gratitude and forgiveness. And while you're reading, share it with others as we all need help in *Our Journey Home*."
JOEY O'CONNOR, Author and Founder of The Grove Center for The Arts

"*Our Journey Home* is a much-needed tool for anyone who wants to get serious about their purity and freedom. I hope believers everywhere will make full use of this material and incorporate it into their churches and their lives."
JOE DALLAS, Author of The Game Plan

The message of *Our Journey Home* demonstrates how it is possible to overcome years of destructive addictive behavior. Zailer manages to honestly and articulately express the feelings of shame, worthlessness, isolation, loneliness and failure that addicts experience. Whether read for personal use or in a group setting, this book illustrates that when people share their struggles with one another, they move themselves into the transformational spiritual process toward true freedom.
JOHN W. KENNEDY, Christianity Today Contributing Editor

"As a mentor and coach to worship leaders and artists, I am grateful for David Zailer and Operation Integrity. *Our Journey Home* is a wonderful tool to help "creatives" who are caught in the mire of addiction and sin find healing for their lives. It's time for us all to get real and embrace the reality of our times! Let's take courage and live in the light!"
MONTY KELSO, Slingshot Group

"Once again, David Zailer brings his personal insights and God-given wisdom to brighten the journey of recovery from the darkness of addiction. If you need insight or inspiration, you need look no further."
LAIRD BRIDGMAN PSY. D, Executive Director of RSA Ministries

It is clear that Dave Zailer's newest work, *Our Journey Home* was written with the Big Book in one hand and the "Bigger Book" in the other. To the reader, proven 12-step principles weave seamlessly with soul-mending messages, whispered from the scriptures. The resulting paragraphs and pages send sanity to the mind and serenity to the heart, borne on the wings of healing and hope. You will start out to read this book, but after a few pages, you will find this book is reading *you*.
TOM THOMPSON, CSAC, Recovery Pastor - Pacific Hills Treatment Center

"A Christ-centered Twelve Step program is not a formula but it is a strategic framework for growth." Those are words in the Introduction of this book that radiate throughout the pages of *Our Journey Home*. Author David Zailer has presented not only the sound principles of Twelve Step recovery, but also unpacks them with insightful biblical understanding, honest personal testimony, and loads of both truth and grace that give rise to a genuine hope of healing and transformation for those who are ready to begin their journey.
DENNY BELLESI, Pastor & Author of The Kingdom Assignment

"David Zailer and the people of Operation Integrity have earned the right to be heard. Faithfully they have worked out their own recovery, supporting one another on their journey, trusting God each step of the way. I strongly encourage you to read *Our Journey Home* with personal reflection, and apply personally the material you hold in your hands."
JIM MASTELLER, Founder of Center for Individual and Family Therapy

"Our Journey Home is another great work by Operation Integrity that guides the reader through real and relevant ways to experience God's intimacy through grace. This is a wonderful tool not only for those reaching for freedom from addiction but for anyone who desires a life changing relationship with Jesus Christ."
COURTNEE SCOTT, President of Distinguished Home Services, courtneescott.com

"Dave Zailer has a gift for integrating Christian truth along with the venerable wisdom of the Twelve Steps. His clear writing makes it easy to read and understand. Dave shares some of the valuable insights that he has experienced in his journey and in his ministry. Now, with this book, these powerful insights are available to everyone who wants to recover from their addictions. This is one of the best resources I have seen. I heartily recommend it to anyone who wants to see God more clearly in the midst of their own recovery journey."
DR. RON SHACKELFORD, CSAT, CSOTS

"*Our Journey Home* is practical application of God's Word coupled with a thoughtful application of the traditional recovery Twelve Steps. This work is an excellent tool for mentoring and can be used as a 365 day personal self-study guide as well. Don't just read this book. Consume it. It is nutrition for the mind and the soul."
TOM YANKOFF, Teacher and Mentor

— author lives in Laguna Niguel!

Our Journey Home

Insights and Inspirations
for
Christian Twelve Step Recovery

Written by David Zailer

in cooperation with

**OPERATION
INTEGRITY**

© 2011 by David Zailer
Published by Homecoming Books
For more information, go to: www.operationintegrity.org
ISBN   10 0615521312
13 9780615521312
Printed in the United States of America

Unless otherwise indicated, Scripture is taken from the HOLY BIBLE, NEW INTERNATIONAL VERSION®. NIV®. Copyright © 1973, 1978, 1984 by International Bible Society. Used by permission of Zondervan. All rights reserved.

Scripture marked AMP is taken from the Amplified® Bible, Copyright © 1954, 1958, 1962, 1964, 1965, 1987 by The Lockman Foundation. Used by permission.

Scripture marked Message is taken from *The Message* by Eugene H. Peterson, copyright © 1993, 1994, 1995, 2000, 2001, 2002. Used by permission of NavPress Publishing Group. All rights reserved.

Scripture marked NASB is taken from the New American Standard Bible®, Copyright © 1960, 1962, 1963, 1968, 1971, 1972, 1973, 1975, 1977, 1995 by The Lockman Foundation. Used by permission.

All references to The Twelve Steps and Twelve Traditions of Alcoholics Anonymous have been reprinted with the permission of Alcoholics Anonymous World Services, Inc. Referencing and reprinting AA quotes does not infer that Alcoholics Anonymous is affiliated with Operation Integrity, Homecoming Books, or any other organization. AA is a program for alcoholism only. And, AA considers itself a spiritual program of action and not a religious organization. Thus, AA is not affiliated with any sect, denomination, or specific religious belief.

Our Journey Home is dedicated to addicted people everywhere, especially those who listen for God's healing invitation to change, transformation, and a better life.

To MELINA,

All the best!!

BREATHE!!! Relax!!!

DAVE

Table of Contents

A Word of Appreciation   xiii
The Christian Roots of the Twelve Steps   xv
The Twelve Steps   xix
Introduction   1
Operation Integrity Prayer   5
Using This Book   7
Chapter One – Step One   9
    Breaking Point   11
    Your Biggest Problem Is You   13
    We Admitted   16
    You Are Not Your Enemy   18
    From Dis-Integration to Integration   21
    God Knows What You Are Going Through   24
    Help Is Available   26
Chapter Two – Step Two   29
    Reaching Out for Healing   31
    When the Blind See   33
    The Power of Imperfect Faith   36
    Healing Hope   39
    It's an Inside Job   42
    Out of the Box into the Light   46
    It's a God Thing   48
Chapter Three – Step Three   51
    Desire   53
    The Decision   56
    Turning Over Our Will   59
    Turning Over Our Life   62
    God as We Understood Him   65
    God Understands Us   69
    Getting Intimate with God   73
Chapter Four – Step Four   77
    Getting a Clear View   79
    Recovering a Healthy Relationship with Ourselves   82
    Who's to Blame?   85
    Truth in Relationship   88
    Seeing the Big Picture   91
    Inner Reality   94
    All Things Good   98

Chapter Five – Step Five 101
    Admitting to God 103
    Jerry Gets Honest with Himself 105
    Becoming Our Friend 109
    Marie's Story 111
    Being the Real Deal 116
    Taking the Next Step 119
    Light Shines Before Us 122

Chapter Six – Step Six 125
    Dissatisfaction and Desire 127
    Ready and Listening 130
    Becoming Ready 133
    What We Really Need 137
    Emotional Triggers 139
    Becoming Aware 141
    Reversing the Past 143

Chapter Seven – Step Seven 145
    From Shame to Grace 147
    Facing the Facts 149
    Humbly Asking 151
    Humility Through and Through 153
    The Source of Our Strength 155
    Changing the Way We Live 157
    Millie Ann's Story 159

Chapter Eight – Step Eight 163
    The Responsibility of Life 165
    The Fundamentals of Forgiveness 167
    Forgiveness – The Way of Healthy Living 170
    Making It Real 173
    The Poison of Resentment 175
    Recovery Is a Gift but It Is Not Free 177
    Moving Forward, Back into Relationship 179

Chapter Nine – Step Nine 183
    Talk Is Cheap 185
    Feeling and Doing 187
    True Forgiveness 189
    An Addict Speaks to His Family 191
    Actions Speak Louder than Words 193
    Proceed with Caution 195
    Life Liberated 198

Chapter Ten – Step Ten   201
    Integrity Inside and Out   203
    A Lifestyle of Vigilance   205
    A Breakthrough for Gary and His Family   207
    The Everydayness of Progress   212
    Complacency and Overconfidence   214
    What God Gives   216
    A Deeper Point of View   218
Chapter Eleven – Step Eleven   221
    A Different Desire   223
    Darnell's Story   224
    Soul Yearnings   226
    Prayer Makes Us Real   228
    Prayer Changes Us   231
    Be Still, Be Quiet, Listen   233
    Priority   237
    The Point of Our Prayer   239
    Recovery Prayers   239
Chapter Twelve – Step Twelve   241
    Destiny Arrives and We Show Up   243
    A New Purpose for Our Lives   245
    Living Life for Others   246
    Possessed by God   250
    Keep Making the Choice   253
    Steve Shares His Life   256
    Questions Remain   262
About Operation Integrity   265

A Word of Appreciation

The family of friends that made this book possible are a very interesting group of people. They come from all walks of life and many different backgrounds. Some don't even know each other. What they share in common is the belief that God is good and that He instills dignity in all people including those of us who have had terrible addictions.

Most of the content and the stories in this book come from the people who are active with Operation Integrity in one way or another. They have names like Mark, Randy, Scott, James, another James, Tom, Mike, Paul, Dick, Don, Jeff, Sal, another Mark, Jerry, Bob, Marie, Steve and Mattie, Gary, Jon-Paul, Rod, Julie, Jim, Tim, Ron, Nancy, Dave, David, Timothy, Judy and Roger, Bryan, Frank, Art, Crystol, Nick, Todd, Rob, Debbie, Charles, Steve, Adam, Stan, Pat, Patty, Andy and Joe. These are people who have battled serious addictions and who are now learning to follow God's call of grace and recovery.

There are others who are not directly involved with Operation Integrity on a day-to-day basis, but who play a supporting role in the development of our organization and literature. They are, among others who are not listed, John and Margaret Snyder from Monarch Beach, California; Jerry Hill from Mission Viejo, California; Ken and Susan Baugh of Coast Hills Church, and many others from Coast Hills Church; John and Patty Kennedy from Springfield, Missouri; and Joey O'Connor from The Grove Center for the Arts and Media.

Operation Integrity works with a network of wonderful therapists from across the United States. We thank all of them for their participation in our work.

The Christian Roots of the Twelve Steps

All Twelve Step Programs can trace their roots to the mid 1930s when Alcoholics Anonymous was founded by Bill Wilson and Dr. Bob Smith, who was a medical doctor and an alcoholic. Alcoholics Anonymous grew out from a Christian evangelical organization called The Oxford Group.

The Oxford Group was founded by a Lutheran minister named Dr. Frank Buchman. Dr. Buchman worked in a variety of capacities over the course of his ministerial career. He worked with the YMCA in Pennsylvania, did evangelistic work in China and directed revival meetings at Princeton, Yale, Harvard, Williams, Smith and Vassar. It was from these revival meetings that local Oxford Group fellowships were established. Wherever they had meetings, The Oxford Group and Dr. Buchman communicated the importance of confessing one's personal resentments and secret "sins" in order to make the most of God's redemption. The local groups organized house meetings which included personal testimonies, witnessing, Bible study and informal discussions. And, additionally, all participants in The Oxford Group were encouraged to reach out and help other people who had problems similar to their own.

In 1934, while still a practicing alcoholic, Bill Wilson received a visit from his longtime friend and drinking buddy, Ebby Thatcher. Ebby had become sober and he credited his sobriety to his involvement with The Oxford Group. A month after this visit, Bill was hospitalized after a serious bout of drinking when Ebby visited him once again. This time Bill was willing to hear about Ebby's experience with The Oxford Group. Ebby told Bill how The Oxford Group helped people change and get over their destructive sins and habits. This became a turning point for Bill Wilson. Once out of the hospital, Bill spent the next three years pouring himself into The Oxford Group, where he learned the importance of the following Oxford Group principles:

1. Complete deflation of the ego and false pride
2. Dependence on and guidance from a Higher Power – God
3. Moral Inventory
4. Confession
5. Restitution
6. Continue to work with other suffering people

It was during his involvement with The Oxford group, and while traveling on business, that Bill met Dr. Bob Smith. Dr. Bob was very hung-over when they first met, and he admitted to Bill that he had previously tried everything to quit drinking but had always failed to permanently stop. Moreover, Dr. Bob thought of his own condition as personal, private, and hopeless. This first meeting between the two men went on for several hours and, by the end of their time together, they agreed they had found a much-needed friend in one another. After one more drinking binge, Dr. Bob got sober and stayed sober. Together, Bill Wilson and Dr. Bob discovered the miracle of how alcoholics can help other alcoholics do what they could not do on their own.

In 1937, Bill and Dr. Bob chose to separate themselves from The Oxford Group because Dr. Buchman had taken on a radical political stance and they felt they should distance themselves from him. This was when Alcoholics Anonymous was born. Even though they had moved on, Bill and Dr. Bob continued to use the basic principles of The Oxford Group along with study of the Scriptures in the early development and growth of AA. In addition, Bill W. encouraged the use of various forms of classic Christian literature as part of one's spiritual nourishment. For example, the devotional guide *My Utmost for His Highest,* by Oswald Chambers, was a book that Bill used for many, many years in his own life.

Over the years AA has evolved into an organization that successfully helps people from all religious backgrounds. At the present time there are approximately 15 million people involved with AA and other Twelve Step recovery groups around the world.

For more information please read:

- *Alcoholics Anonymous Comes of Age* from AA World Services
- *Courage to Change – The Christian Roots of the 12-Step Movement* by Sam Shoemaker, Hazeldon Publishers

The Twelve Steps

Step One   We admitted we were powerless over our addiction, that our life had become unmanageable.

Step Two   We came to believe that a Power greater than ourselves could restore us to sanity.

Step Three   We made a decision to turn our will and our lives over to the care of God as we understood Him.

Step Four   We made a searching and fearless moral inventory of ourselves.

Step Five   Admitted to God, to ourselves and to another human being the exact nature of our wrongs.

Step Six   We became entirely ready to have God remove all these defects of character.

Step Seven   We humbly asked Him to remove our shortcomings.

Step Eight   We made a list of all persons we had harmed, and became willing to make amends to them all.

Step Nine   We made direct amends to such people wherever possible, except when to do so would injure them or others.

Step Ten   We continued to take personal inventory and when we were wrong, promptly admitted it.

Step Eleven   Sought through prayer and meditation to improve our conscious contact with God as we understood Him, praying only for the knowledge of His will for us and the power to carry that out.

Step Twelve   Having had a spiritual awakening as the result of these Steps, we tried to carry the message to others, and to practice these principles in all our affairs.

Introduction

Recently, I was participating in a newly formed Operation Integrity Recovery Fellowship. This new fellowship came to exist just like all Operation Integrity fellowships come to exist. A small and growing group of motivated men, all coming together to help one another recover from addictive behavior.

Sitting there, I listened to these men share their experiences, both past and present. And as I listened, I was reminded of how Operation Integrity originally began. OI began in 2001 as an informal group of men who started meeting together to help themselves, and one another, rise above and heal from past sins and sexual indiscretions. We didn't have a name for our meeting then. We just showed up and kept showing up. The number of people who came to our meeting grew and as our numbers increased we began to believe that we were involved in something very special. We sensed God's loving hand on our lives and in our meetings. We were no longer just a group; we had become a fellowship.

The more I attended these meetings, the more I realized what good people the men in this fellowship were. Now don't get me wrong, these guys were some serious sinners, and I know a sinner when I see one because they usually look a whole lot like me. However, what was most amazingly obvious to me was a subtle, yet profound goodness in each of them. I could hear from what they shared about themselves that, along with their moral failings, there was a kind of organic dignity and worth inside each of them. These men could not be described in simple terms like good or bad. They had a powerful dignity that was all human, as shown by their obvious flaws and shortcomings, and more than human at the same time because each of them, myself included, showed an instinct to want more out of life than what we could provide for ourselves. Even more, we felt a calling that was urging us to become more than what we knew how to be. We were huge sinners and we were reaching out for an intimate connection, a connection that only God can satisfy.

Our fellowship became a formal organization in 2004 when we became Operation Integrity. Our purpose in Operation Integrity is to help men and women recover from addiction, leading to radical transformation of their lives. We work to guide others in developing *a recovery program of action* that is empowered by God through an intimate encounter with Jesus Christ and other people. At the center of everything we do at Operation Integrity is the belief that God exists and that He is interested in having a meaningful relationship with all people. We believe that God has the human face of Jesus Christ and if you want to know God, you can know Him through an honest encounter with Christ.

Today, Operation Integrity is realizing many opportunities that we did not first envision. We started, and we remain, an organization that is committed to helping people recover from sexual addiction, but our message is reaching out to help all kinds of people with all kinds of addictions. Many of the people who benefit from Operation Integrity today are not addicted to sex in any way. Some use our literature as part of their Twelve Step program for other addictions. Others use our material and take part in our fellowship because it helps them dive deeper into the intimate grace that God gives through recovering people. While we will never forsake our original development as a Christ-centered Twelve Step program for sexual integrity, we will share the goodness that God has given us with you and anyone who feels they may benefit from it.

A Christ-centered Twelve Step program is not a formula but it is a strategic framework for growth. While specific results cannot be guaranteed as to exactly how one might change, the changes that happen in those who are dedicated to working a program like this are dramatic and amazing. When we couple our honest desire to change with a Christ-centered recovery program and fellowship, God always shows up and He brings His miracles with Him.

The following pages are a collection of thoughts and awakenings that come from people who are involved with Operation Integrity in one way or another. The common bond we share is our need for God and our need to deal with our shortcomings and our addictions responsibly.

David Zailer

"I pray that from his glorious, unlimited resources he will empower you with inner strength through his Spirit. Then Christ will make his home in your hearts as you trust in him. Your roots will grow down into God's love and keep you strong. And may you have the power to understand, as all God's people should, how wide, how long, how high, and how deep his love is. May you experience the love of Christ, though it is too great to understand fully. Then you will be made complete with all the fullness of life and power that comes from God."

- Paul, the Apostle, Ephesians 3:16-19, *NLT*

Operation Integrity Prayer

I pray that I will learn to desire obedience more than blessing or comfort and to know that the greatest blessing in life is to live obedient to your will. May I learn to better give up my will and find my complete and total satisfaction in your will. My self-centeredness destroys me but seeking you and doing your will brings life to me. Realizing this, I have decided that my mind, my heart and my will, will be directed to you. I will find my purpose and identity in knowing you more personally and living more powerfully according to your Spirit.   Amen

Using This Book

It should be noted that the suggestions we make regarding the use of this book come from what we have learned through our own personal Twelve Step recovery experiences. We do not consider ourselves uniquely qualified to instruct anyone about their walk with God. We are just sharing with you what has worked for us. Here are the things we have done that have helped us in our recovery:

- **Involvement in a Twelve Step fellowship** for a minimum of 3 to 5 years. These meetings should be attended as often as possible.
- **Individual Twelve Step work with a sponsor**. This is where we develop a lifestyle which may be referred to as *A Spiritual Program of Action.*
- **Family involvement in the recovery process** through Al-Anon or a similar recovery fellowship. This is to support and educate family members of those who have addictions.
- **Meeting regularly with a qualified counselor or therapist** for a minimum of 3 to 5 years.
- **Treat the underlying issues that contribute to addictions**. These include but are not limited to: abuse suffered in childhood, depression, a sense of hopelessness or meaninglessness, narcissism, toxic shame, stress, loneliness or feeling alienated, unresolved anger, and unhealthy social or family relationships.

These are things we have done that helped us deal with ourselves and our addictions responsibly. And, as we responsibly deal with our addictions, we are better able to recognize how God deals lovingly with us. God's love changes us into the kind of people who are just not interested in our addictions anymore. And, more than anything, it is the grace of God that compels us to share our recovery experiences with others.

The purpose of this book is to help you recover from addiction and grow roots that are deeply embedded in the love of God. It can be used for devotional reading, as a discussion tool for recovery groups or as part of your existing recovery program. However you choose to use it, you must understand that reading this book will not give you recovery. Only God does that. Recovery will be yours only as you surrender your life to Him and work to make the most of the help He brings to you.

There is a very good chance this book is part of that help. Read it with an open mind and a humble heart. Look for things you have in common with the people who are sharing their stories in this book and try not to look for the differences. The more you relate with the people and the content of this book, the more you will benefit from it. Read this book often. And once you finish it, tell another person how you feel about it.

Yours in Christ and recovery,

The Men and Women of Operation Integrity

Step One

***We admitted we were powerless over our addiction,
that our life had become unmanageable.***

Step One can be characterized as experiencing a deep and absolute sense of personal failure because we have repeatedly failed to get our addictions under control. It is hitting a bottom physically, emotionally, or spiritually, or maybe even all three. In Step One, we admit that our addictions are stronger than we are. Our ego has been conquered. In a very deep way, we know that the pain of staying the same will be far greater than the fear we feel about changing.

Perhaps the most difficult thing for us to see is the increasing destructiveness of our addictions. Some of us will see this and admit it and others of us will not. If we don't see this now things will probably get worse for us because of how the destructive nature of addiction progresses over time. One thing is for sure, our bottom can always go deeper, right up until we die.

Step One calls us to surrender and give up a fight that we have been losing all along. It must be done with the full conviction of heart and mind otherwise all of our efforts to recover will be wasted. In admitting that we are powerless over our addictions and that we cannot presently manage our own lives we gain the initial foundation that we need to do a turnaround, and begin the process that will eventually lead us to overcoming our addictions.

Both in addiction and recovery, pain is one of our greatest motivators.

Breaking Point

"What I don't understand about myself is that I decide one way, but then I act another, doing things I absolutely despise. So if I can't be trusted to figure out what is best for myself and then do it, it becomes obvious that God's command is necessary. But I need something more! For if I know the law but still can't keep it, and if the power of sin within me keeps sabotaging my best intentions, I obviously need help! I realize that I don't have what it takes. I can will it, but I can't do it. I decide to do good, but I don't really do it; I decide not to do bad, but then I do it anyway. My decisions, such as they are, don't result in actions. Something has gone wrong deep within me and gets the better of me every time."

Romans 7:15-20 *The Message*

"We perceive that only through utter defeat are we able to take our first steps toward liberation and strength. Our admissions of personal powerlessness finally turn out to be firm bedrock upon which happy and purposeful lives may be built."

-Alcoholics Anonymous

We admitted we were powerless over our addiction, that our life had become unmanageable.

Addictions destroy people. They are a kind of self assault, a personalized form of self execution. Some addiction experts have called it "suicide on the installment plan." Inevitably, we hurt ourselves with our addictions, usually without even realizing it. We bring destruction to our bodies, our relationships, our careers and we harm ourselves in unseen ways via the emotional and psychological self-wounding which come from repeatedly doing the things that we know are not right to do. Perhaps the greatest harm done is the spiritual damage we suffer when we violate our own standards and ethics of conduct and morality.

Without help, addictions always progress as demonstrated by the ways we have increasingly violated our own sense of right and wrong. And, without help, we can lose to our addictions our own sense of identity— that is, a realistic view of who we are and how our lives are being lived out. Even our own ability to make healthy choices can be stolen from us by our addictions. It's not like we don't know the difference between right and wrong, it's just that addiction overwhelms us, robbing us of the power to consistently live well. It works out like this: We know what is right and we want to do right, but in the end we find that we have done the wrong thing and we usually have no reasonable explanation as to why we did the wrong thing and not the right thing, which is what we really wanted and intended to do. Looking back we've always known in our heart what was right and we never wanted to do what was wrong. Moreover we certainly never meant to become addicted to anything. However, in the light of honesty we will also remember how we've made repeated promises to ourselves, and others, only to break our promises many times over.

The Apostle Paul, who some call the greatest Christian who ever lived, offers us an insightful perspective that can be used as a sort of universal detection device for addictions. In Romans 7:15 Paul says, "What I don't understand about myself is that I decide one way, but then I act another, doing things I absolutely despise." What the Apostle Paul tells us in Scripture can help us to understand that it is possible for anyone to suffer from an addiction and even the greatest among us, like the Apostle Paul, will only escape their powerlessness if they are willing to recognize it and admit it.

Amidst this difficult reality there is a bright spot. Admitting our powerlessness over our addiction is the end of our aloneness and the beginning of our recovery journey. But, unless we admit that we need help and we become willing to receive the help that is available to us, things will only get worse, they will never get better. Without help, our addictions will always get worse, never better.

Your Biggest Problem is You

"It's the way you've lived that's brought all this on you. The bitter taste is from your evil life. That's what's piercing your heart."
Jeremiah 4:18 *The Message*

"If, instead of failing, the person temporarily succeeds in stopping the addictive behavior, the greatest mind trick of all comes into play. It starts out very normally, with the natural joyfulness of liberation. 'I can do it! I have done it! And it wasn't even that difficult! Why, I actually don't even have any desire for a drink anymore. I'm free!' Before long, the natural joy will undergo a malignant change; it will be replaced by pride."
- Gerald G. May, M.D.

We admitted we were powerless over our addiction, that our life had become unmanageable.

Many of us have had the painful experience of having our weaknesses exposed and then being punished for those weaknesses. As a result, we've often developed a protective veneer of polite and subtle dishonesty. We usually don't lie outright, we just don't tell the truth about ourselves when we should. For us to admit that we were powerless over our addiction and that our life was unmanageable meant admitting defeat. And it was. We were defeated by our addictions whether we admitted it or not.

Admitting a personal defeat is counter to everything most of us have been taught. Culturally, in very subtle ways, we are brought up to be people who are determined, self-sufficient and strong. But, in the revealing light of addiction there is one absolutely essential question that needs to be answered: Are you going to recognize and are you willing to admit that your addictions are more powerful than you are?

For most of us, our upbringing instilled in us the instinct to try harder when we failed, and that we should never admit defeat, discouragement or weakness. This often turns into a stubbornness that can lead people with addictions into a continuous downward spiral of pride and failure and control. The more we've been determined to control ourselves, the more we failed. By refusing to admit our personal insufficiency, we pridefully puffed ourselves up and became determined to control ourselves better the next time. When we failed again, which was almost certain, we became all the more obsessed to control our life and the lives of others. Inevitably, the obsession to rule our life and the lives of others brought on more pride, which brought more failure, and addiction ruled all the more. Pride, failure and control are the building blocks of denial, which is the pride based bedrock of addiction. In denial and pride, our self–willed efforts to control our lives and others become one of our greatest liabilities.

So, we have to be willing to admit that we have been defeated by our addictions if we are going to recover from them. As counterintuitive as it appears to be, when we admit our powerlessness it becomes possible for us to transcend our powerlessness because we become open to solutions that we could not see through the eyes of denial and pride. When we get honest about our powerlessness it becomes possible for us to find solutions to the problems that we could not solve on our own. It's not like we become stronger; it's more like we are infused with a strength that is made available to us when we get honest. The power does not come from us. It comes from outside of us but connects with us on the inside. With this outside power coming in to us we get lifted up, from the bottom up. As we admit our addictions and powerlessness, we become part of a movement of change that is bigger than our own efforts could ever be. We move into solution. The cycle of pride, failure and control gets interrupted. Failures are no longer as fatal as they once were. When honest about them, our failures can become a small step sideways and not the inevitable free fall to the bottom that they were before.

We don't need to make promises in our admissions and confessions. We just tell the truth about ourselves, the best we know how to do. We say it like it is. After all, we are only human. There is great dignity and freedom in being honestly human.

We Admitted

"If you think you know it all, you're a fool for sure; real survivors learn wisdom from others."
> Proverbs 28:26 *The Message*

"When we have accepted the worst, we have nothing more to lose. And that automatically means – we have everything to gain."
> -Dale Carnegie

We admitted we were powerless over our addiction, that our life had become unmanageable.

Everything that we do in a worthwhile recovery effort begins with "we." We cannot allow ourselves to be alone if we hope to have a worthwhile recovery experience, because no one recovers from their addictions alone. We have to have help. While each of us will have a different story to tell, all of our stories end up pretty much the same way: addicted.

In our addictions, we become isolated by our secrets and by our shame. We feel guilty about the things we've done and we feel shameful about the secrets we've kept. We often feel like we are little more than a huge mistake that must be kept hidden from others at all costs.

In our efforts to combat our sense of aloneness, many of us have participated in various groups that were based on commitments of religion, social service, virtue, promise keeping, and faithfulness. We participated in these groups with full sincerity, always working with great diligence so we would not fail. We thought that if we could make ourselves to be of great importance we could solve our own internal pain. But we could not. Our best efforts were never good enough for us. No matter how much we excelled in our good works, our own sense of failure continued to grow. Whatever we did, no matter how good or worthwhile it was, it was never good enough. We thought we had to be perfect. It seemed to us that if we could get it right, whatever it was, then we could get ourselves right too. We always worked harder. To us, things were never good enough. We became perfectionists. Then, we would even find failure in our greatest achievements. Strange as it sounds, no matter what the successes we achieved, or the failures we experienced our addictions seemed to become ever more attractive. And, paradoxically, the harder we worked to overcome our addictions on our own the more our addictions ruled our lives.

Left with few, if any, viable opportunities for change we admitted we needed help. And, we took the first step in getting help by seeking out a recovery fellowship, a place where it was safe to admit that we were not in complete control of our lives. Desperate, we admitted that we had been unable to overcome some very serious problems with our behavior and that our life was beyond our ability to manage. In making our admission, we began to set aside our own ego-centered independence in order to seek out a connectedness and fellowship that could do for us what we had not been able to do for ourselves. Alone we are dying, but together we can recover and live.

You Are Not Your Enemy

"I live in disgrace all day long, and my face is covered with shame."
Psalms 44:15 *NIV*

"Growth begins when we accept our weakness."
-Jean Vanier

We admitted we were powerless over our addiction, that our life had become unmanageable.

If we want to recover from our addiction, we will have to be willing to undertake a new journey. Starting out, it's not very likely that we will know exactly where this new journey will take us. Certainly we will have hopes, and probably a few expectations, too. It is, however, very important that we maintain an open mind regarding our hopes and expectations, because it is very easy for us to put ourselves in charge of our recovery without even realizing it. At this point, to take charge of our own recovery would be just another extension of our addictive and self-controlling ways that have always gotten us into trouble. So, as we set out on our journey, it's important that we stay focused on the day-by-day and step-by-step process. Doing this will help us to stay away from our addictions and, by putting one foot in front of the other, move a little further down the recovery path each and every day.

Our recovery journey starts with getting honest. It is essential that we get honest about how we think and feel about our lives, ourselves and other people. When we get honest with ourselves about our lives, it becomes possible for us to see healthy changes in our relationships, most specifically our relationship with our own thoughts and feelings. This will in turn affect, in a healthy way, our relationship with ourselves, our lives and other people. As these relationships improve they will, over time, help to build healthy and affirming thoughts and feelings inside of us, which will help to displace the destructive and self- condemning thoughts we have suffered up to now. As this happens we will begin to see everything about us change for the better, beginning at the most personal and intimate level of our thoughts and feelings.

As we got honest, most of us expressed how we have often suffered deep feelings of shame. Shame has been described as a feeling that one is fatally flawed and undeserving of happiness. Some have described their feelings of shame as the feeling and belief, as in conviction, that they were just one big mistake. In shame, we think and feel like everything about us is horribly wrong or fatally flawed in some way. In shame we can feel like the world would be better off if we weren't around.

Shame can be one of the most destructive feelings a human being can experience and shame is often a catalyst for our addictions. Much of the power of our addictions comes from an internal drive that seeks to overcome, to escape from, or compensate for feelings of shame. Unhealed shame guarantees that our life will be unmanageable.

Shame is nothing new, it's been around as long as people have been around. Even in the Bible, written thousands of years ago, the Psalmist wrote from his heart, "I live in disgrace all day long, and my face is covered with shame" (Psalms 44:15 NIV). So you see, we are not the first to suffer shame and we will not be the last. Fortunately, shame can be addressed. It can be made a useful and helpful, but probably not enjoyable part of our lives.

One man who we know from Operation Integrity described his feelings of shame in this way:
"From my earliest childhood, whenever I would see a picture of myself I would immediately feel sick to my stomach. Looking at me I would see someone of great disgust. I thought I was s _ _ _. Sometimes I could barely keep myself from throwing up. It didn't matter what the picture was, who I was with or what the event was, seeing myself I would get sick. These feelings continued until I was in my mid-forties. Then, thank

God, I got help. It was in about my second year of my recovery from my addiction and working the steps that I realized that I was no longer feeling as I had felt before. Somewhere along the way of the process I realized that I was okay. Today I feel good about having my picture taken. I can see myself, and even when it is a 'bad' picture, I'm okay with it all."

Step One is the place where we can put on the brakes and begin to turn the corner and find a new direction for our lives—not only for our addictions but also for the pain, the shame and the suffering that has given power to our addictions.

As we honestly work through our Twelve Step journey with others in our recovery fellowship, we will begin to understand the components which have built the deep shame that's troubled us. Recognizing shame, getting honest about it and accepting it for what it is, is the first step to effectively deal with it. Dealing with shame is similar to dealing with our addiction. We accept our weakness, we admit it and we ask for help. In doing so we discover the key to changing it. We move from shame to grace and from death to life.

From Dis-Integration to Integration

"I've lost twenty pounds in two months because of your accusation. My bones are brittle as dry sticks because of my sin. I'm swamped by my bad behavior, collapsed under gunnysacks of guilt. The cuts in my flesh stink and grow maggots because I've lived so badly. And now I'm flat on my face feeling sorry for myself morning to night. All my insides are on fire, my body is a wreck. I'm on my last legs; I've had it - my life is a vomit of groans."

> Psalms 38:3-8 *The Message*

"What helps at this point is to see your consequences as your teachers. You have been sent a lesson to learn. If you don't learn the lesson this time, it will manifest itself again, and probably in a more painful form the next time."

> -Patrick Carnes, Ph.D.

We admitted we were powerless over our addiction, that our life had become unmanageable.

As we battled alone against the progressive nature of our addictions, we experienced a general *disintegration* of our lives. Our lives get worse, never better. Many of us have expressed how we've felt that we were getting sicker and sicker every day that we battled our addictions alone. No matter how valiant and determined we were—and still are—the war has continued to rage. And, much to our chagrin and embarrassment, we have been losing the battle.

In Scripture, which is the historical backbone for everything that we believe as Christians, there are examples of people who suffered because they lived selfish lives. The result was a life that became destructive for them. For example, the psalmist David, who was called a man after God's own heart, gives us an example of someone who, even though he had previously experienced deep intimacy with God, found his life *disintegrated* because of his selfish way of life.

In Psalm 38 that we reviewed above, David's words speak to us regarding the physical consequences, the guilt and the resulting shame and self-pity that come from living life in a destructive way. We don't know exactly what it was that was causing David's distress, and that's really not so important right now. What is important is to realize that we, along with David and everyone else, will experience inevitable consequences as a result of the way we live our lives. The consequences of a destructive life, as much as we would like to deny it, manifest themselves in failing health and an overall loss of life, especially in our relationships.

David found that it was time to ask for help. He did this by admitting that he was powerless over his problems and that he was not qualified to manage his life. A little later in the same chapter from the Psalms, David continues to say in verses 21 and 22, *"Don't dump me, GOD; my GOD, don't stand me up. Hurry and help me; I want some wide-open space in my life!"*

The lesson for David, as it needs to be for all of us, is that we will bring calamity upon ourselves when we run our life independent of God and contrary to what we know is right. Also, David helps us to see that when our lives are shattered as a result of our own mistakes, it is never too late to ask God for help and mercy.

As Christians, we know that God created *us,* but God did not create our addictions. Our addictions are a result of the way we have lived our lives. This is not to say that we are totally at fault for becoming addicted because none of us ever meant to become addicted to anything. Sometimes addictions can be a genetic misfortune that, when coupled with the first taste of an overwhelming temptation, take hold of a person with a life-consuming power. While we are not totally at fault for having an addiction, we are wholly responsible for our addiction and for reaching out and making the most of the help that is available to us. Neither God nor anyone else is responsible for our addiction or for our recovery. None of us will ever recover if we expect someone else to do it for us. Complaining and pointing fingers will never help us recover from our addiction or anything else. To recover, we have to be willing to surrender our lives, and no one can surrender our lives but us.

For most of us, surrendering our addiction and asking for help has been the most difficult thing we have ever done. No matter how hard it was, we had to. We really didn't have any other good choices left. If we wouldn't admit that we needed help, we could not move from the *disintegrating* life of addiction into the *integrating* life of recovery.

God Knows What You Are Going Through

"As He saw many people, He had loving-pity on them. They were troubled and were walking around everywhere. They were like sheep without a shepherd."

> Matt 9:36 *New Life Version*

"To be alive is to be addicted, and to be alive and addicted is to stand in need of grace."

> -Gerald G. May, M.D.

We admitted we were powerless over our addiction, that our life had become unmanageable.

Step One of the Twelve Step recovery process requires that we get honest about how we have failed to control our addictions and our lives. This includes recognizing and admitting that we have lost control over our compulsive desires and that we have failed in all of our attempts to regain control.

To recover from our addictions, it is important for us to recognize that no human being, no place, or anything else will solve our internal problems. In fact, even our own efforts will become problems for us if we rely on them alone to change the way we think and feel about ourselves and our lives. Even the little nagging personal problems that we have but don't consider as addictions (mostly our bad habits, our secret fantasies and our illusions) will take on the qualities and destructive aspects of addiction when we rely on them. After all, addictions are nothing more than bad habits that have become both idolatrous and pathological. In the end, only God can do for us what we have been unable to do for ourselves.

At the center of everything we believe as Christians is a belief that God has the human face of Jesus Christ. Through the scriptural story of the life of Jesus, we see how God reacts to people when they suffer. God, through Jesus, responds to suffering with compassion and empathy. Compassion, commitment to love, and empathy are the displayed characteristics of the God-humanness that was and is the life of Christ. As God walked the earth through the life of Jesus, He never turned away from anyone who asked Him for help. Now it is important to understand that not everyone that encountered Jesus came away from meeting Him with the kind of help that they wanted. There were, after all, those who had violent reactions to Jesus and there were also those who came away disappointed and unhealed. But, to those who were willing to admit their hopeless suffering, Jesus gave a power and grace that changed the way they viewed themselves and their lives. In their sincere confession, they were given a power to change that had not been available to them before they met Christ. Hopelessness was made into faith, and suffering made into strength. While God does not offer us an escape from inconvenience or discomfort, He does offer us a complete and total change of who we are, which in turn will change our life. To experience this change, we must first admit our anguish and longing which then opens us to a desperate but powerful faith and hope in God's love and care.

Step One is the prelude and preparation for a life-changing faith and hopefulness. First, we must admit that we cannot solve our problems on our own, no matter how hard we try. As we do this, we get in touch with the center point of our pain and desperation, which is the exact place where we became willing to ask God to do for us what we could not do for ourselves. With God there is hope, and without Him we're screwed.

Help is Available

"He will rescue the poor when they cry to him; he will help the oppressed, who have no one to defend them. He feels pity for the weak and the needy, and he will rescue them."

> Psalm 72: 12-13 *NLT*

"People see God every day. They just don't recognize him."
> -Pearl Bailey

We admitted we were powerless over our addiction, that our life had become unmanageable.

Those of us with addictions tend to be great actors. We attempt to keep our outsides looking really good so that no one would suspect that we're all messed up on the inside. Sadly, nothing could be further from the truth because, in the final analysis, our secrets and addictions prove that we've been little more than pretenders. Mostly, we've been going through life acting like we are in control and that our problems happen because other people are not behaving as they should. We've generally had an attitude like we've got it all together, and if the rest of the world would just cooperate with us, then everything would be okay. Do you recognize the thinking here? We fake it. We pretend. We go through life with a head full of fanciful thinking. We are selfish.

Inadvertently, we have made ourselves to be our own god. We have worshiped our own lives, our own agendas, our own priorities and our own values. In short, we have valued ourselves above all else. And many of us have actually done this covertly by hiding ourselves in religion. Whatever we call it, the result has been the same: addiction. So, we find ourselves in a tough spot. We have to make a change in our thinking and in our attitude because the old ways just don't work anymore.

Recovery from addictions will only come to those of us who can acknowledge and admit that we cannot manage our own lives. As long as we are too proud to admit our weaknesses, we will never be able to change them. If we are going to live and recover, we will have to find a belief and a faith in something that will work for us, because what we've had up to this point hasn't been working. Has it? We need to have help from a Power that is greater than we are. A Power that can heal us where we could not heal ourselves, from the inside out. In light of the destruction that addiction has brought us, we must know that we'll be better off cooperating with this Higher Power instead of trying to overcome it or deny it.

While it is true that we will need help from other people along the way, our failures to heal ourselves prove that we must learn that only God will be the ultimate solution for our problems. Sometimes as we ask for help we must make the simple and difficult admission of our fearfulness, as well as our powerlessness. On the one hand we fear God and His unpredictability, and on the other hand we fear our addictions and their certainty.

Our problems have not really been our addictions, or even the painful circumstances of our unmanageable lives. We—our own self-centeredness, that is—is really our major problem. Only God, who often works through people, can solve the "you" and "me" problem and give to us the liberation we've been created to experience. As we put our hope in God, we find that our past humiliations become humility for today. As we hope and trust in the Higher Power, God can make the tragedy and weakness of addiction into a joy that positively empowers everything we think and feel and do with our lives. As faith in God becomes real for us, we find that our addictions and our lives become helpful and encouraging to others as well. After all, everyone is addicted in one way or another.

Step Two

We came to believe that a Power greater than ourselves could restore us to sanity.

Step Two is the logical outgrowth of Step One. When we truly want to recover from our addictions, we'll reach out with an open mind in order to get the kind of help that will stop the downward spiral of our addictions.

Step Two is about recognizing new ways of thinking and living, new ways to succeed where we had failed. We come to understand that there is a solution for every problem and that we can find these solutions when we're open-minded enough to see it. When the student is ready, the teacher will show up.

Step Two is not about church or religion, although church and religion may play a role. This is more about learning to relate to God and other people in very personal, trusting and intimate ways. It's important to understand that we'll never relate to God in a way that satisfies until we're willing to recognize how we have in the past been playing God ourselves, usually without even realizing it. And before we can relate to God and other people in healthy ways, we'll have to be willing to become abstinent from our addictions. Or, at the very least, bring them into a healthy balance. This includes matters related to money, sex, career, hobbies, food, medications, chemicals, relationships and social interests. If we are unable or unwilling to surrender these addictions now, we move in that direction by admitting our lack of surrender. Recovery is always possible when we are willing to get honest.

Reaching Out for Healing

"Jesus answered them, 'Healthy people don't need a doctor—sick people do. I have come to call not those who think they are righteous, but those who know they are sinners and need to repent.'"
>   Luke 5:31,32 *NLT*

"Grace strikes us when we are in great pain and restlessness....
Sometimes at that moment a wave of light breaks into our darkness, and it is though a voice were saying: 'You are accepted.'"
>   -Paul Tillich

We came to believe that a Power greater than ourselves could restore us to sanity.

It is not likely that anyone will visit a doctor when he is healthy. It's only the weak and suffering who need a doctor's care. In the past we have denied the sickness and suffering in our lives, but in Step One we admitted our problems and we accepted the fact that we could not manage our lives on our own. After all, the pain from our addictions is what has motivated us to get help. Furthermore, we have to be honest with others if we really want to recover. We must honestly admit our problems in order to get the help that will empower us to change. Only a crazy person would go to a doctor and then not be honest about what he really needed.

God is the Great Physician, the One who will ultimately heal us from our addictions. In Scripture we have a historical record of how God has healed the sick and suffering through the person and life of Jesus Christ. In Jesus, God never turned away from those in need. When people in pain came to God with their hopeful sincerity, He always responded by healing them. Jesus, in giving God's grace, not only cured the outer illnesses, He healed internal illnesses as well. The healing that Jesus offered to others helps us to understand that we are loved and accepted by God, and that His love and acceptance is available to us even before we knew that we needed it. As God heals us internally, spiritually we receive an empowerment that helps us to heal emotionally and psychologically. Spiritual health and psychological health go hand in hand. This hand in hand kind of health is the unifying, integrating work of grace.

Today God continues to work through human beings. Just as Jesus heals us for eternity, there are people who can help heal us in our day-to-day lives. In order for us to recover from our addictions, it is necessary for us to seek out and accept help from various God-given resources like medical doctors, mental health professionals and recovery support groups. These people and organizations are the most common ways that God helps us recover from our addictions. They are to us on a day-to-day level what Jesus is to us on the eternal and spiritual level. As God through Jesus heals us internally, these people help us to see the acceptance of God, and His love and healing become a reality in our lives every day. Remember, no one recovers alone.

When The Blind See

"As Jesus was leaving town, trailed by his disciples and a parade of people, a blind beggar by the name of Bartimaeus, son of Timaeus, was sitting alongside the road. When he heard that Jesus the Nazarene was passing by, he began to cry out, 'Son of David, Jesus! Mercy, have mercy on me!' Many tried to hush him up, but he yelled all the louder, 'Son of David! Mercy, have mercy on me!' Jesus stopped in his tracks. 'Call him over.' They called him. 'It's your lucky day! Get up! He's calling you to come!' Throwing off his coat, he was on his feet at once and came to Jesus. Jesus said, 'What can I do for you?' The blind man said, 'Rabbi, I want to see.' 'On your way,' said Jesus. 'Your faith has saved and healed you.' In that very instant he recovered his sight and followed Jesus down the road."

Mark 10:46-52 *The Message*

"It's really very simple, either God is going to save me, or I'm screwed."

-Robert Orman

We came to believe that a Power greater than ourselves could restore us to sanity.

Enmeshed into and promoting all addictive behaviors is a self-defeating and destructive way of thinking. It's the way that we've seen ourselves and life as a whole that has been the problem. This includes inaccurate and distorted personal beliefs and self-centered agendas that send us time and again into insane activities. With this in mind, we can begin to see that our problems are deeper than our behaviors; our problems are how we perceive ourselves and life as a whole.

We all can change the outside of our lives temporarily, but changing the insides has been impossible up to now. As we get honest about our addictions, we can begin to see that some of the most pervasive damage done to us has been the result of a way of thinking that was closed-minded, selfish, and chronically frustrated and negative. At best our lives have been a groping around in darkness. At times we would see something that we thought would help us, and grasped for it only to find that it was nothing more than a vapor or a shadow. Life was always getting worse, never better. We were dying a little more every day. God wants to change all this.

In Mark 10:46-52 we read about a blind man who encountered Jesus and came away having had his blindness healed. This blind man, whose name was Bartimaeus, can be our guide as to how we, too, can find our blindness of perspectives healed and made whole by God. Bartimaeus' blindness was apparently physical, where ours is more a spiritual and psychological blindness. But the principles that we need to apply to our lives are the same. Bartimaeus, when he heard that Jesus was coming down the road, abandoned his place, and in "throwing off his coat" made a mad dash to seek out Jesus. It seems that Bartimaeus was hungry and desperate for healing. This desperate hunger, along with a hopeful belief that it was possible for Jesus to help him, caused him to take decisive action. Bartimaeus' belief in the possibility that his life could be made whole drew an amazing affirmation from Jesus himself. Jesus said, "Your faith has saved and healed you."

This is what it can be like for us. As we come to believe that it is possible for our lives to be different, God, working through others, can heal us, giving us renewed sight to see perspectives of sanity and health. Our lives will be different. We can be healed. We will be healed. Most likely it will not be an instantaneous healing like our friend Bartimaeus had, but a healing restoration of sanity nonetheless. Most often the healing we experience will be a developing process where our spiritual eyesight improves over time. As we seek out the help that God provides, we will—one day at a time—experience increasing clarity of thinking and a growing sense that our future will be bright, happy, joyous and free. Furthermore, as we accept the friendship of the blind man and as we place our hope in Jesus, we come to believe that God loves to heal the blind.

The Power of Imperfect Faith

"What do you mean, 'If I can'?" Jesus asked. "Anything is possible if a person believes." The father instantly cried out, "I do believe, but help me overcome my unbelief!"
　　　　Mark 9:23, 24 *NLT*

"When I was driven to my knees by alcohol, I was ready to ask for the gift of faith. And all was changed. Never again, my pains and problems notwithstanding, would I experience my former desolation. I saw the universe to be lighted by God's love; I was alone no more.
　　　　-Bill Wilson

We came to believe that a Power greater than ourselves could restore us to sanity.

Coming to believe that we can be restored to sanity is an expression of faith. Faith, which is often confused with religious tradition, is more of a trust and confidence than anything else. Faith is more personal than religious, although faith may be a part of one's religious convictions. Whereas many of us have previously experienced religion as a controlling set of rules that masquerade as belief, faith is more of a fundamental confidence that leads to effective, life-giving action. Religion is doing things in an attempt to make ourselves right. Faith is believing that God is *making* us right, and this leads us to *doing* what is right. This is not to say that faith doesn't play a necessary role in religion, because it does. Religious people of all kinds express their faith in ways that help keep them mentally and emotionally balanced. The ways that healthy people, religious or not, live out their faith are lessons that are essential for us to learn as recovering addicts.

Faith is a trust—a trust and confidence that can be known as a deep abiding conviction of the heart and the mind. A deep abiding conviction of faith is the foundation of a healthy and happy life. It integrates the heart and the mind. Faith that is real is the abiding belief that God can and will do for us in our recovery what we have been unable to do on our own, no matter how hard we tried. Faith is a reaching out, an opening of the mind and the heart to possibilities that we had ignored or opportunities that we had refused in the past. In faith we trust in God and we trust in the people that God brings into our lives who can help us in our recovery. In faith we come to believe that God will provide all that we need to recover and that our responsibility is to simply supply the honesty, the openness and the willingness to do the work of recovery. In faith, God provides everything that we need to recover. In faith we know that if He doesn't provide something that we think we need, we accept that we don't really need it after all.

Real faith is honest and in touch with reality. It never defies the facts. Our friend that we read about in Mark 9, verses 22 and 23, gives an honest expression of his heart and his mind. On the one hand he cries out desperately, hoping for help for his son and at the same time expressing the weakness of his faith. He seems to be torn but really he's just being human. Jesus recognized that, amidst his struggling expression of faith, this man was really expressing a faithful struggle of hope and belief. Jesus knows that our honest faith is never without doubt. From this story we can learn to have faith in God's empathetic care. We can have faith that Jesus, who the Bible says is God in human form, understands what it means to be human. He understands the struggle of faith, the faithful struggle to believe that God will connect to our weak faith all the power and resources necessary to accomplish His healing love and care in our lives. Our friend in this story seems to understand this, and it is necessary for us to understand this as well.

In Step Two, we are putting our faith in God and not in ourselves, which would lead us back to our addictions. Faith in our own faith is nothing more than wishful thinking and superstition. In Step Two we just believe, as faithfully as we can, that God will come through for us. It's really very simple. A weak faith that trusts in a loving and powerful God is more than sufficient to meet any of the demands that we will face in our recovery. And, as we struggle faithfully to believe in God's care and love, we can know from this scriptural record that Jesus will carefully give us all that we need, just as He did for our friend. Our faith doesn't need to be perfect because our faith is in God. He takes care of the rest.

Healing Hope

"He was teaching in one of the meeting places on the Sabbath. There was a woman present, so twisted and bent over with arthritis that she couldn't even look up. She had been afflicted with this for eighteen years. When Jesus saw her, he called her over. 'Woman, you're free!' He laid hands on her and suddenly she was standing straight and tall, giving glory to God."

> Luke 13:10-13 *The Message*

"Hope is a risk that must be run."

> -Georges Bernanos

We came to believe that a Power greater than ourselves could restore us to sanity.

Faith is the antidote for and the antithesis of addiction. Where addiction kills, faith gives life. Along with our deep desire to survive our addictions, hope came alive inside of us. This hope brought with it an open-mindedness that we had never had before. As we looked to others in our fellowship who were recovering, and combined that with our own desire to survive our addictions, faith was born. It took root inside of us. Even before we asked for it, a hopeful faith appeared quiet and close— coming from outside of us, but connecting and working within. As we saw others recover from their addictions, *we came to believe* that we could possibly recover, too. Our hopelessness changes to hopefulness as we honestly connect with others.

In Luke 13 there is a story about an amazing woman whose suffering was healed as a result of her hopeful faith coming in contact with God. We don't know a lot about this woman. We don't even know her name. So, to help us become friends with her, let's give her a name. We'll call her, Esperanza. Esperanza suffered for eighteen years with what was apparently a very painful and deforming illness. From the story, we know that her illness was increasingly robbing her of her ability to function in life as she normally would have. Her body had become so bent and mangled from her illness that she had lost the ability to look up. Do you know how that feels?

We can imagine that, along with her bodily illness, Esperanza suffered unrelenting sadness, depression and anxiety as a result of the ongoing pain she felt from her illness. We can surmise that, under the crushing weight of mental and emotional fatigue, Esperanza was unable to raise herself up emotionally and spiritually. And we can assume that our friend Esperanza also suffered deep regret over the loss of many opportunities, shame due to her deformities, and self- loathing due to the feeling that she was no good to anyone any more. Does this sound familiar to you? Whatever hopefulness and fortitude that she had on her own was obviously not enough to help her. Her reality was that she was stuck and things were getting worse, not better. Can you relate?

While our addictions have probably not brought on the degree of physical suffering that Esperanza endured, it is important for us to identify with her suffering. After all, addictions are physical diseases just as much as they are emotional, mental and spiritual diseases. Over time our addictions erode us physically, sometimes to the degree that our bodies will never be the same again. And we suffer in more than physical ways, too. Among these sufferings are shame, regret, and self-loathing. When all is said and done, pain is pain. No matter what form that the pain comes, it hurts. In our addictions we were, like Esperanza, stuck and painfully waiting for help.

Referring back to the Scripture in Luke, we will notice that this story takes place in or around one of the meeting places that the religious people of the day frequented on their day of worship. Specifically, the Scripture tells us that Esperanza was 'present' in this location. This is an interesting insight for recovering addicts, because it is important for us to remember that it is essential that we keep ourselves in places—both physical and spiritual—where God is the center of our attention. By being present in the meeting place on the Sabbath, Esperanza was keeping herself in a place where recovery was possible for her. She was doing all that she could do, all the while waiting for and being present to the possibility that a savior and healer would come along. There was nothing more that Esperanza could do to help herself. So, she did what she could do. This is how Esperanza displayed her faith.

This is what is important in our Step Two. First, we come to believe that we can be restored to sanity. Then, we come and be part of a fellowship with others who are recovering from their addictions. Most of all, we stay alert. We stay emotionally and spiritually present to every opportunity to reach out and touch back to the hand of healing when it comes our way. All the while, we remain as open-minded as possible, because we are not exactly sure when the healing touch will come or through whom it will come. Like Esperanza, we stay open in our faith, being as "present" as we can to fellowship and hope. Simply said, we maintain an attitude of hopefulness the best we can. We stay ready to receive the touch that will make a difference in our lives. We stay, like Esperanza, emotionally, spiritually and physically present. In this way we become ready to be touched, connected, integrated and healed. It will not likely be a physical touch like the immediate healing Esperanza experienced. It will more likely take the form of help through our recovering fellowship, a doctor or a counselor, but it will be a healing nonetheless. By the way, Esperanza is a Spanish name that, when translated into English, means *hope.*

It's An Inside Job

"The Spirit can make life. Sheer muscle and willpower don't make anything happen. Every word I've spoken to you is a Spirit-word, and so it is life-making."

John 6:63 *The Message*

"This life therefore, is not righteousness, but growth in righteousness, not health but healing, not being but becoming, not rest but exercise. We are not yet what we shall be, but we are growing toward it: the process is not yet finished but it is going on. This is not the end but it is the road; all does not yet gleam in glory but all is being purified."
-Martin Luther

We came to believe that a Power greater than ourselves could restore us to sanity.

When we talk about recovery, what we are really talking about is a deepening of a person's integrity. In Webster's dictionary, integrity is defined as a completeness, a unity, soundness, personal honesty and independence. For the purposes of recovery, let us think of integrity as a healthy condition of the soul. Integrity is sanity—a condition of sanity that incorporates completeness, unity, soundness, personal honesty and independence in that we are not dependent on any person or thing in a way that's destructive for us.

Ultimately, addiction and integrity cannot exist together, although they do exist to some degree in the reality of each of our lives. Where addiction takes root in the small cracks and crevices of our hearts and minds, and then splinters us even more, recovery heals this split, bringing integrity and sanity back to our lives. Recovery is an interpersonal coming back together, a reintegrating of our heart and our mind together, as one.

To illustrate this, let us tell you about a friend of ours named Mike. Mike restores old pickup trucks for a hobby. What he does with these old trucks is an example of what we do in our recovery. First, Mike starts by considering the overall condition of the truck, evaluating the best he can what needs to be done to make the truck new again. Then, with help from others, he begins the process of dismantling the truck, cataloguing each part as he goes. Every piece is closely inspected by Mike and his restoration partners. Broken or damaged pieces are either discarded for new pieces, or they are repaired as necessary. Because Mike has learned that he can't do it alone, he's had to learn where to go to get the help he needs when he needs it. Sometimes it's a welder, sometimes a painter or a mechanic or an upholster. Whatever help he needs, he asks for it.

Now, there comes a time where the process begins to reverse itself. Mike, with help from his friends, begins to put the parts back together again. Each part and piece are reconnected together according to the original builder's design. When the work is done, an incredible process has been undertaken, more than any one man could ever do on his own. The old has been made new again. All of the originally designed pieces have been renewed and reintegrated back into proper alignment with one another. *The process was restoring an old truck but the end result is a new old truck.* For you see, no matter how good a job Mike and his friends have done, it could never be more than the original designer had intended. Furthermore, without the original designer's intent, Mike and his friends, and all of their combined efforts, could never make what the truck has become in its restoration.

Here is where Mike's hobby can guide us. We are solely responsible for doing our recovery work. It is our job to reach out and ask for help. No one can do for us what only we can do for ourselves. Just like Mike with the truck, we have to learn where to go to get the help that we need when we need it. This is where our "higher powers" come into play. We all have "higher powers" in our lives. Employers, parents, family, doctors, governments, law enforcement—each has power to control and influence our behaviors. These are external powers that can effectively influence what we do and how we do it. In the recovering community there are Twelve Step programs, medical and mental health professionals, plus there are sponsors and recovery mentors who have experienced their own restoration of sanity. Each of these can help us in the "heavy lifting" of our personal restoration. And while this help is essential, it will not be enough. It should be noted that even the best of helpers can only do so much for us. They themselves will still lack some degree of integrity. They are only human, after all.

So, this is what it looks like. We, with help, do our recovery work, but it is God—working through people—that restores sanity and integrity to us. In recovery, we can say that today we are better integrated than we were yesterday or the day before. And, the greatest indication that integrity is growing in us is that we develop an increasing inclination to admit where and how we lack integrity. We can never make this kind of growth on our own. It only comes from the One who made us. Similarly, what Mike and his friends do is great, but even with all the work they've done in the restoration process, they did not make the truck. That was done before they ever came along. There was an original Master Planner and Builder who made the truck to begin with. Really, all that Mike and his friends have done is to bring the truck back to what it was originally made to be.

And so it is with our lives. We are an original, one-of-a-kind that is described in the Bible as being "created in the image of God." Believing that we can be restored to sanity means to live out our lives in a spiritual way. In times past, we lived like we were physical beings trying to become spiritual, or religious as some would say. In reality, we are spiritual beings first and we are living out our lives in physical ways. Being spiritual obviously does not make us perfect, as proven through our ever-present good intentions that so often end up in ways we did not intend. In the balance of this spiritual and physical life that we live, we are ultimately responsible for our own work of recovery, and at the same time we can only be restored to sanity by the work of an ultimate "Higher Power" that we call God.

At the end of the day, sanity is an integrated life that is lived according to an authentic faith in God. This authentic faith is born inside of us as we are, in our spirit that is touched by God's Spirit. It's simple really. We do what we can and God does the rest. As we are willing to work and trust, which is faith in action, God gives us the Spirit of Life who brings life to our efforts and sanity to our lives. After all, it was God who formed us.

Out of The Box and Into The Light

"I am Light that has come into the world so that all who believe in me won't have to stay any longer in the dark."

John 12:46 *The Message*

"Pay attention to the external Source and the internal power will be there."

-Oswald Chambers

We came to believe that a Power greater than ourselves could restore us to sanity.

Most of us have had our addictions much longer than we first realized. Because of the destructive impact that our addictions have made on our hearts and minds, we've probably not known what it means to be emotionally healthy. It's like we've grown up being locked away in a box. There—in our addictions, that is—it would be impossible for us to see the light of freedom. Without light we could not see the future with any sense of joy or healthy expectation. Living in addiction is like being stuck in a cave for so long that we have forgotten what it feels like to have the warmth of the sun on our face. Because we've only known the dark up till now, it's been impossible for us to comprehend The Light.

But, as we get connected to a recovery fellowship, we begin to see people who have seen "The Light" and the hopefulness that the Light brings with it. From the example of others whose lives are being changed for the better, we can see how things can change for us—that the destructive patterns of our lives need not continue anymore. With what we can see in the Light, we come to believe that change can happen for us because we see it happening for others right before our very eyes. This is how God, the Higher Power, works. He works through people.

As God gives us the Light, through the guiding direction of others, we begin to see the pathway to recovery and change being illuminated right in front of us. We see that the Light for living is available to everyone. We find its usefulness not because we are special, but because it is the nature of light to illuminate things around it. Our job is simply to put ourselves in the light, which is another way of saying we put our confidence and trust in God. For many of us this was a radical but subtle departure from the ways we have talked about God in the past. Let's get honest; simply talking about God really hasn't helped us much in the past, has it? After all, many of us have spent much of our lives in religious exercise, but have never known God as any kind of real Higher Power. If anything, our addictions prove that in the past God, as we would refer to Him, has been little more than a religious symbol or relic, impersonal words on a page of religious material, or possibly for some of us, a tyrannical overlord that demanded that we observe religious impositions that seemed to be irrelevant and arbitrary.

For God to be the Light—our Higher Power, that is—means to recognize God as the One that we trust will show us the way to a life that is free from our addicted insanity. Then, in faith, God, the Higher Power, becomes our Protector, our Sustainer, and our Redeemer. If we think of God in any way less than this, we take Him for granted. And if we take God for granted, we waste this chance to recover from our addicted insanity. Either God is the ultimate Higher Power for us or He is nothing for us.

Furthermore, as God works in our lives, we find that the Light that illuminates the way for us is not always pleasant. Not only does the Light shine the way to a hopeful future, but it illuminates areas of our lives that we have not considered before. Many of these areas will need to be changed just as much as our addictions need to be changed. In his loving care for us, God does not discriminate.

It's a God Thing

"I will love You, O LORD, my strength. The LORD is my rock and my fortress and my deliverer, My God, my strength, in whom I will trust; My shield and the horn of my salvation, my stronghold. I will call upon the LORD, who is worthy to be praised; So shall I be saved from my enemies."

Psalm 18:1-3

"The strength of a man consists in finding out the way in which God is going, and going in that way too."

-Henry Ward Beecher

We came to believe that a Power greater than ourselves could restore us to sanity.

Medical doctors call addiction a disease because it embeds itself into our bodies physiologically, creating dependencies that have definitive symptoms. Psychologists will often refer to addiction as "attachment," because in addiction we become "attached" to things in ways that are destructive to us. Religious teachers often call addiction idolatry and sin because of the way that addictions skew our personal priorities. Because addiction can be seen from differing points of view, it is important for us to understand that each viewpoint has merit because addiction affects the whole person—physically, mentally, emotionally and spiritually. Addictions hook our bodies by creating biochemical dependencies in our brains. It takes hold of our lives by creating attachments to people, places and things that we addictively think are necessary for us when they really are not. And, our addictions keep us from having a meaningful connection with God because we value the things we are addicted to more than we value God. Whichever viewpoint is considered, the result of addiction is the same. Lives erode and people die in one way or another.

It has been said that addiction is the most human of all diseases. After all, addiction has been around since man has been around, and in one way or another we are all addicted to something. In the past, addiction has affected us physically, mentally, emotionally and spiritually. But we don't need to stay addicted any longer. When we become willing to seek a spiritual solution to our addictions, we will begin to find solutions for the physical, mental and emotional problems as well. The willingness to look for a new kind of spiritual solution is a kind of grace. We say it's grace because, as we admit that we need help and in coming to believe that we can be restored to sanity, the downward spiral of our addiction has been interrupted. This is something that we could not do on our own.

Furthermore, by grace we have the opportunity to take steps that will help heal us. This is a decisive dignity that we had once lost to our addictions. Somehow, by grace, at the precise point where our hopeless desperations collide with the hopeful desire to find sanity for our lives, we'll find a decisiveness that we didn't have before. Because the pain of staying the same was more than the pain of changing, we decided, without even realizing it, to reach out and grab onto what we've come to believe will restore sanity to our lives. Seeking to recover from our addictions, through the power of grace, we seek the kingdom of God, which means to simply make God the King of our lives. For you see, the kingdom of God is nothing more than the place where God is King.

Remember our friend David from Psalms 38:3-8? Some believe that David had serious problems with addiction. We don't know for sure, but it's possible that David may have been addicted to sex. Considering how he pursued a sexual relationship with Bathsheba, who was a married woman, and how he orchestrated the circumstances where her husband would be killed in order to hide his sexual impropriety, there is evidence to the real possibility that David was addicted to sex. Most poignant of all is that he seemed to be in deep denial of the consequences of his actions. David, like any addict, was blind to see how his actions were hurting others.

To David's credit, when his wrongs came into the light, he felt a deep need to change. He not only realized how wrong his actions were, but he also realized that he had unwittingly become—because of his addictions—his own worst enemy. This helps to explain how David, as he wrote in the Psalms, "I'm on my last legs; I've had it - my life is a vomit of groans," had found himself at a decisive crossroads. He realized, as we have, that his life was unmanageable and he needed to change in order for his life to change. David was, as we are, at the crossroads of faith and decision. The ultimate question for David—as it is for us as well—is what will the future be like? David, in Psalms 18:1-3, tells us how he expressed his willingness to reach out and connect with a Power that would make a difference in his life.

Our friend David would not allow his addiction to define his entire life, though there was no escaping the consequences of his past. He decisively committed in his heart and mind to seek out a relationship with God. In so doing, David began to find a new and healthy identity for himself. Ultimately, David came to be known as a man after God's own heart, even in spite of his addictions. The same can happen to us. As we come to believe that we can be restored to sanity, we gain the opportunity to discover and live out a whole new identity. It's an identity and life that is a perfectly scripted plan for our lives by the design of a loving and caring God. The possibility to live this miracle is here. The only question for us is, will we be willing to live it out?

Step Three

We made a decision to turn our will and our lives over to the care of God as we understood him.

When we combine the desperation that we admitted in Step One along with the hope that we find in Step Two, we will realize that the most sane thing to do is to give ourselves over to God's care. We give Him control and care over every aspect of our lives. He is, after all, more than a religious conversation piece. He is the ultimate Higher Power, the absolute Essential for life.

This means that we turn everything over to Him, including our recovery, our families, our jobs, and even the little things like a broken car or appliance. In Step Three we remove ourselves out from the center of our focus and we put God there. We are no more important and no less important than anyone else. And, above all, we understand that God is more important than anything or anyone.

The key to Step Three is willingness. It is not a once-and-for-all decision. It is the kind of decision that we make every day, the best we can. And, all the while, we freely admit any struggles we face in making this decision of surrender. Remember, no matter how far we move forward in recovery, recovery only starts and progresses as we admit that we are not in control and that we need help from God and others.

Step Three is where we decide who we will become in life and what our life will be like from here on out. Step Three is where the miracle begins.

Desire

"If you are tired from carrying heavy burdens, come to Me and I will give you rest. Take the yoke I give you. Put it on your shoulders and learn from Me. I am gentle and humble, and you will find rest. This yoke is easy to bear, and this burden is light."
　　Matthew 11:28-30 *CEV*

"I am seeking, I am striving, I am in it with all my heart."
　　-Vincent van Gogh

We made a decision to turn our will and our lives over to the care of God as we understood him.

As we battled our addictions alone, it seemed like we were always failing. The harder we tried to overcome them on our own, the more they stole life and dignity from us. Over time, our addictions even began to erode the greatest of our God-given dignities: the ability to make clear and correct personal choices for ourselves. Time and again, our addictive obsessions promised freedom but instead they gave us an ever-increasing load of guilt and shame. Burdened by guilt and shame, we often chose to follow our addictions where we fell, once again, deeper into addiction. But no more! Things can change for us now. Today we stand at a crossroads. In one direction are the addictions that we've loved so much. In the other direction lies a new kind of life where our addictions will no longer be the center of our world.

In Step One we admitted just how stuck we really were. Then it was in Step Two that we realized that our lives could change if we were willing to rely on a power that was greater than we were. The place where Step One and Step Two meet is a kind of spiritual intersection, an intersection of choice for our lives. With addiction in one direction and faith in a Higher Power in the other, the only thing left to be decided is which direction we are going to go. Do we want to live or die? This choice no one can take from us, or make for us. For you see, the real battle of recovery is won or lost in the battle of our will. Will we be self-directed—which is how our addictions have taken hold of our lives—or will we be God-directed and recover from our addictions? The battle for recovery is won or lost in the private places of our will, where only we and God really know what is going on with us. It's never in full view of the world. Even the empowering desire to recover that we are experiencing is a gift from God, who has already grabbed hold of us, compelling us to get alone with Him and surrender our lives to Him. Until we do this, we will lose every time.

Remember our friends from Scripture, Paul, Bartimaeus and Esperanza? All of them, at the point where their own sense of powerlessness intersected with their hope for healing, found within themselves the desire to put their faith in God who, through Jesus, had made himself available to them. Empowered by the desire for change, they made the decision to trade in their powerlessness for the powerfulness that Jesus had displayed to them and to others. This was not a religious decision for them. We doubt that they even considered it as anything more than a desperate appeal for help, which is exactly what it was. After all, they really were not "doing" anything. They were simply making the only reasonable decision that could be made when everything else had failed. And the same is true for us, too. In light of the combined desperation that we feel in Step One and the hopefulness we begin to experience in Step Two, the decision to surrender ourselves to God's care becomes the most simple and sane thing we can do. Like our friends from the Scriptures, the record of our own addicted life will give us many good reasons to want to trade in our own powerlessness for the powerfulness that Jesus has displayed in the lives of people as historically recorded for the past 2,000 years.

If we want to recover, all we have to do is decide in whom we are going to put our trust and confidence. Will we continue to trust only in ourselves, or will we decide to put our life in God's care? What we choose to do with our will is the single most significant and personal decision we will ever make. We are ultimately responsible for making the choice of what our lives will be like, what kind of people we will be and to whom we will belong. This decision can never be taken from us. We can no longer escape it. We are forever responsible for it. It's a simple question really, one that we face everyday. Who will you trust? Who will you follow? Will it be your addiction or will it be God?

The Decision

"If any of you want to be my followers, you must forget about yourself. You must take up your cross and follow Me. If you want to save your life, you will destroy it. But if you give up your life for Me, you will find it. What will you gain, if you own the whole world but destroy yourself? What would you give to get back your soul?"

Matthew 16:24-26

"To gain that which is worth having, it may be necessary to lose everything."

-Bernadette Devlin

We made a decision to turn our will and our lives over to the care of God as we understood him.

It has been said that everyone will have their Waterloo. In addiction we have found ours, too. We can no longer deceive ourselves, or anyone else for that matter. Our addictions have been profound. We know it, and other people know it. Because of this, we just don't have the energy to go on the way we've been going. Physically, mentally, and spiritually we're done. It's all over. It's the end. It seems that we're as good as dead. But here, when we're at the end of ourselves, there is a calling for us. God, the giver of life, is calling for us to accept the loss of our own lives in order to accept the life that He has to give us.

The decision to surrender ourselves to God's care is far more personal and practical than religious. We surrender our will and life to God because if we continue to live as we have, our addictions will destroy us. We've simply come to understand that God is a life-or-death decision for all of us. And today, each of us decides whether we are willing to trust God or continue our journey alone. Failing to trust leaves us spiritually alone and unprotected against our own progressing addictions. This is a potentially fatal mistake for anyone who has an addiction.

When we decide to trust God, we are not making a religious decision, although many religions encourage us to do this as well. You see, it's not religion that we need. If religion was the answer for our addictions, those of us who came from religious backgrounds would never have had the addictions that we've had. What we really need is intimacy with God. Intimacy with God is far more personal than religious. It is an intimacy that transcends all that we are as human beings. Intimacy with God puts God inside of us. It makes us bigger than what we could ever be on our own. We call it a surrender because we can't be exactly sure how this intimacy with God will affect us. But while we may not know exactly how God and His goodness will play out in our lives, we do know that it will be far better than staying in our addictions.

Ultimately, all of us will stand before God with their future literally in their own hands, making their life decision for themselves in their own personal way. Some recovering addicts, when they made their decision to trust their life to God, experienced immediate and profound gratitude with dramatic emotional outbursts. Others experienced only a quiet sense of relief that their life would change. Whatever the experience is for us as individuals, each of us must understand that it is far better to make the decision to surrender and trust than continue on the way we were going. We know that we must have God's help and we have decided to ask for it.

As we make the decision to surrender our lives to God, let's pray in ways that are personal and intimate. Let's pray like this:

Dear God,
Only You are God and I am not. You are the Maker and Fulfiller of life.
As for me, I know that I originate from You, that I exist because of You.
Today, I make the decision to give myself to You, the best I know how.
You own me, as far as I am concerned. I am Yours. I give You my old life
and I ask for You to give me Your life. You can do with me anything You

want to do. Now there are times when I get deceived and I become distracted from You. When I do, I feel that You are far away and I am hurt, from the inside out, when I sin. But, according to Your Word and Your promises, I know that You are always with me. Only You can save me from my addictions and my sins, renewing me in the center of my soul, my will. You protect me, You save me, You transform me. I thank You for the changes in me that You have promised. I want to be more of Yours. I seek You, and by Your grace I am finding and knowing You. It is my desire to know You more intimately and to more effectively live out the life You have for me. Amen

Turning Over Our Will

"With all your heart you must trust the LORD and not your own judgment. Always let him lead you, and he will clear the road for you to follow."

> Proverbs 3:5-6 *CEV*

"We deify our independence and self-will and call them by the wrong name. What God sees as stubborn weakness, we call strength."
>   -Oswald Chambers

We made a decision to turn our will and our lives over to the care of God as we understood him.

Everyone is addicted to something. While some things are more addictive to some people than others, the potential is there for all of us because of the biochemical connections that happen in our brain and our bodies. In fact, we can potentially become addicted to things that are not even thought of as addicting, because addiction has more to do with the inside of us, than it has to do with things that are outside of us. For example, let's say that we have become addicted to jelly beans. Now we all know that jelly beans are not generally considered as addictive, but, nonetheless, it is possible that we may be so profoundly affected by our love of jelly beans that we begin to think and feel, at least to some degree in our psyche, that we "need" jelly beans. Being addicted to the jelly beans means that we've come to believe that they are necessary for us. We think that we need them to be happy and to maintain what we think is normal for us. This is the way that addiction corrupts our priorities, misplacing other things that are truly more important.

Just like with jelly beans, we can potentially become addicted to any person, to any place and to anything. The addictions we've struggled with have embedded themselves into our priorities and our intentions and, in doing so, they've hijacked our desires. The sum total of our priorities, our intentions and our desires equals our will. This means that ultimately we get addicted in our will.

The will is best described as what we intend on doing and what we plan to do. Perhaps we can best understand the term "will" if we think of it as our focused desire, our commitment to pursue, the giving of our attention, what we most deeply desire. Our will is what we want, what we pursue, with what and how we devote our attention. It's what we are committed to doing. It's what we really want. It connects us to everything we hope and dream for. It's connected to our personal history including family, career, love interests, even religion and politics. Our will reveals everything we really think and feel about ourselves, other people, and the world in which we live.

In the past we have lived by our own willpower. And, as our addictions prove, our self-determined willpower has entangled us, getting us attached to people, to places and to things in ways that are not healthy for us. If we become attached to people, to places or to things in ways where they become more important to us than God's will, our willpower is weakened accordingly. The more we exert our willpower for our own self-centered desires, the less effective it becomes. This is where the bondage of addiction gains its deadly toehold in our lives. Even though we often don't realize it, the root of our addictions—and our sins, too—is pride. Willpower alone will never be enough. It must be empowered by God.

The antidote to our pride and our addictions is humility. Turning over our will to God's care is the ultimate, and intimate, humility that only we can do for ourselves. What we are really doing is turning over every thought, every feeling, every desire, and every intention. We don't try to change them ourselves, and we certainly don't deny them. We just admit them and then turn them over to God. It doesn't matter whether they are good or bad, we turn them over either way. As we turn over our will, even in the smallest of ways, our struggle with addiction begins to be—to the degree of our surrender—consecrated by God. As we turn over our will and our life to God, our personal will begins to be made holy.

Let us never forget that God is fully connected to everything we think and feel. He knows it all and He doesn't turn away. In knowing all, He calls us home to health and recovery. This journey home begins with a letting go of our attachments, which is a way of allowing God to become fully involved in our thoughts and feelings. As we turn over our thoughts and feelings to God, they begin to become transformed by God. The power of God's grace flows into us most freely when we decide to align our will with God's will. As we do this, God will become more important and we will become less important. This simple decision is the most powerful way that any human being can exert his or her will. It is our choice for our recovery. It's evidence of the initial transformation of everything we are, beginning with what we want and hope for, our will. Some of us prayed in this way:

Dear God,

I pray that I will learn to desire obedience more than blessing or comfort and to know that the greatest blessing in life is to live obedient to Your will. May I learn to better give up my will and find my complete and total satisfaction in Your will. My self-centeredness destroys me, but seeking You and doing Your will brings life to me. Realizing this, I have decided that my mind, my heart, and my will, will be directed to You. I will find my purpose and identity in knowing You more personally and living more powerfully according to Your Spirit.

Amen

Turning Over Our Life

"Those who live in the shelter of the Most High will find rest in the shadow of the Almighty."
　　Psalm 91:1

"The world is not to be put in order, the world is in order. It is for us to put ourselves in unison with this order."
　　-Henry Miller

We made a decision to turn our will and our lives over to the care of God as we understood him.

Once we have made the decision to turn our will over to God's care, we'll quickly learn that it's impossible to do so without turning our life over to God's care as well. We simply can't do one without the other. The way we live life is the truest indicator of our will. Until we give our life over to God, we have not surrendered our will, no matter what we think or say.

This has been our problem: we've considered our personal wants and wishes as entitlements and necessities, and because of this we've been making demands on God and others in ways that we do not realize. When we fail to get what we want, we become angry and resentful, which is proof that we have not turned over our will and life to God's care. Anger and resentment expose us as the self-centered people that we are. Sometimes, even without realizing it, we punish others in one way or another, and in so doing, we can become so intolerable that those around us will leave us or send us packing. When we create these kind of situations for ourselves, our personal misery grows all the more, making our addictions attractive once again.

In one way or another we've fought the world and everyone in it. We have, at times, become like mercenaries. We've fought for what we thought was important. If pushing and shoving didn't work, we kill 'em with kindness in order to hide our selfishness. Sometimes we claimed victory and gloated in ever-so-subtle ways. Other times we politely admitted defeat, apologizing for our behavior just to regroup and try again. Attitudes like these are indisputable evidence that we have even become addicted to our own self-image, the image of what we think our life is supposed to be like. Without knowing it, we became addicted to what we thought our life was supposed to be.

With all this in mind, the next order of business for us is to give God our hopes, our dreams, our expectations, all of our agendas, even the way that we have thought about ourselves and our life. After all, whatever we thought our life was supposed to be like in the past hasn't really been working, has it?

In true surrender to God, we quit fighting anyone or anything. We recognize that the only battle worth fighting is within ourselves. We turn our hope over to Him and make it His hope. We give Him our dreams. We give Him our problems and we allow them to become His problems. We make our expectations the expectation of God's gracious working in our hearts and our minds with all other considerations as secondary. We determine ourselves to act, the best we can, according to what we know to be acts of love for God and love for others. We give up our agenda in order to live according to His agenda. Everything about us becomes His. Our life is no longer ours to run. We have given it over to God, and our life will be what He determines it to be. Not easy, but simple.

Because we are powerless over people, places, and things, we make it our only goal to live out a faith that longs for God and hopes for His care. With this "turning over" we fulfill our eternal calling. It's the ultimate decision of faith, the most dignified thing we can do in this life. It's not just another image we've made for our lives, because we no longer claim ownership of our lives. It's bigger and more open-minded than that. It's a decision that acknowledges all of our own efforts and resources are insufficient. The turning over of our life is our personalized declaration, a God-given dignity, in which we state unequivocally that we are worth far more than we can ever give ourselves credit for. And yet, we have no need to claim any importance because with this decision—this dignity—we realize that we are made for bigger things than we could ever think or imagine on our own.

In the dignity of faith we are now consciously saying what we have been unconsciously saying to God in countless areas of our lives. We want Him and we know that we cannot live without Him. God has always known this and now we know it, too.

Serenity Prayer - attributed to Reinhold Niebuhr

God grant me the serenity to accept the things I cannot change; courage to change the things I can; and the wisdom to know the difference. Living one day at a time; accepting hardship as a pathway to peace; taking, as Jesus did, this sinful world as it is, not as I would have it: trusting that You will make all things right if I surrender to Your will; that I may be reasonably happy in this life and supremely happy with you forever in the next. Amen

God As We Understood Him

"This is how much God loved the world: He gave His Son, his one and only Son. And this is why: so that no one need be destroyed; by believing in Him, anyone can have a whole and lasting life. God didn't go to all the trouble of sending his Son merely to point an accusing finger, telling the world how bad it was. He came to help, to put the world right again."

John 3:16-18 *The Message*

God, I offer myself to Thee, to build with me and to do with me as Thou wilt. Relieve me of the bondage of self, that I may better do thy will. Take away my difficulties, that victory over them may bear witness to those I would help of Thy Power, Thy Love, and Thy Way of Life. May I do Thy will always! Amen

-Third Step Prayer from Alcoholics Anonymous

We made a decision to turn our will and our lives over to the care of God as we understood him.

I am not God and neither are you. We must fully accept this simple fact if we are to ever have an effective and workable understanding of God.

As children, seemingly from birth, we tend to think that everyone and everything around us is connected to us. As we grow up a little, we come to realize that we are separate from the world and only part of a larger context, but we still tend to think of the world in relationship to ourselves. It's like we are the center of our own universe. We feel good when the world—the people, the places and the things around us—gives us what we think we need. But when the world doesn't cooperate, we tend to feel bad and then we try to change the world so that we can feel better. This has never worked for any of us. No matter how hard we've tried, we cannot control the people, the places, or the things around us all of the time. Because we believed that it was so important for us to be in control of our world, and because we invariably failed to control this world of ours, we could never provide any sense of security or well-being for ourselves. No matter how hard we tried, we could not do what only God can do.

No matter how good or bad we feel, or what degree of success or failure we experience, one thing is for sure: things are going to change. God is the only constant. He is the only reality. The lives that we know are only temporary. The only way that we will ever experience any relevance or permanence in our life is through a relationship with God. As we understand that no one is God but God, we can begin to experience life in a way that transcends not only our addictions, but all of our other failures and shortcomings, too. This is because our life, including all of our addictions and failures, becomes lost in the life that God will give to us. We'll no longer be the center of our world. That job belongs to God and no one else.

When we really think about it, understanding God is a contradiction in terms. He is beyond our comprehension, after all. But, because of the way God made us, our hearts can know what our minds cannot. God—who is the ultimate above and beyond and more than us—through the working of his Spirit meets us within us, in our spirit. As God comes from the outside of us and works within us, we receive on the inside of us what was needed in order to move up and beyond the addictions that have kept us down for so long. In short, God is the complete other than and more than what we can do in our own efforts. God will do for us what we cannot do for ourselves.

In our addictions, we had become attached to things in ways that are destructive for us. When we rely on our attachments (whatever they are) to make us feel okay, we expect more from them than they can ever really give to us. God, however, is the perfect attachment, because He is not addictive in any way. While the attachments that we made in our addictions end up taking more than they give, making an attachment with God will always give to us more than we can ever need. Besides, all that we are really giving to God is our addicted life, and He gives back to us a life that is free, complete, and eternal in every way. When God is the center of our world, our life and world get put right, in order, complete, and powerful. Our relationship with God is the only relationship we will ever have that cannot become addictive or unhealthy in any way. This is because God is totally good. He cannot corrupt us because there is no corruption in Him. He cannot become unhealthy for us because He's not unhealthy in any way. Sometimes, religious pride or indoctrination masquerades as God. This happens when it is based more on human intellect and reasoning than on faith in God himself. When this happens, religion becomes nothing more than religious posing and faking, which is both highly destructive and addictive. If it is unhealthy or addictive, it is not of God. Sadly, religious addiction is perhaps the most insidious of all addictions.

Scripture is a rich history that tells us that God loves people who have addictions. God not only loves people *like* us—he likes *us,* too. He delights in the way we yearn to experience life in the most full way. Individually, He loves us and wants us no matter who we are or what we've done. We know this because there are people who've been addicted like us and who have discovered God's love for themselves. Thankfully, an authentic relationship with God is not a matter of how smart we are, but how sincere we are with Him. He takes care of the rest. It's simple, it's effective, and it's the way God is.

All of us, whether we recognize it or not, need God. We all need to know that someone is loving enough and powerful enough to perfectly love and care for us in the ways that we really need. Jesus is the one Person who has always known God in this way. Jesus reveals to us who God is and what He is like. God will never be exactly what we want Him to be, but He will always be what we truly need Him to be. Throughout history, as recorded in Scripture, there has been only one person whose life displayed perfection of purpose, whose death exemplified the perfection of love, and who had the power to live again after death, which has changed the course of world history and our own addicted lives. This is Jesus. Unlike all other human beings, Jesus was not addicted to anything in any way. Jesus had all of the same human attachments that we all have, but He never became addicted to his attachments because He put His full confidence in God, and God alone. Because His life was fully centered around God, the entire scope of Jesus' life was free.

Through Jesus, God embraces everyone who wants to be embraced. Showing this through the scriptural record, God—as He was living through Jesus—even forgave those who were attempting to destroy Him. Scripture tells us in Luke 23:34 that he even expressed love for those who were killing Him, because He knew and understood that they just didn't know or understand who He was or what He was all about. After giving up His life, Jesus lived again. As He appeared to His followers, He declared once and for all that He is the One who is capable of giving life to addicted and dying people like us.

Jesus lived His life close to those who were, just like us, in desperate need of Him. In so doing He calls us to himself, to His love and to His God our Father. It is in Jesus that we can have confidence for life and recovery. Through Him we are empowered to live.

God Understands Us

"O LORD, you have examined my heart and know everything about me. You know when I sit down or stand up. You know my thoughts even when I'm far away. You see me when I travel and when I rest at home. You know everything I do. You know what I am going to say even before I say it, LORD. You go before me and follow me. You place your hand of blessing on my head. Such knowledge is too wonderful for me, too great for me to understand!"

     Psalm 139 :1-6

"So in terms of what every man needs most crucially, all man's power is powerless because at its roots, of course, the deepest longings of the human soul is the longing for God, and this no man has the power to satisfy"

    -Frederick Buechner

We made a decision to turn our will and our lives over to the care of God as we understood him.

Knowing that God knows us through and through can be very troubling. Nevertheless, our friend David from the Psalms didn't seem to mind. He even expresses joy and amazement knowing that God is so aware of him. We might think that David would feel this way because of his self-confidence. This may be partly true because David was a man of great success, but he was also a man of tremendous failure, too. It's more likely that David's joy came from his belief that God had a loving and careful interest in him—the kind of love and care that didn't depend on whether he was a success or a failure.

David's experience reminds us that no amount of virtue, religious or otherwise, will make us immune to temptation, to sin or to failure. To his credit, David honestly faced his failures, and as he did so he experienced an expanding relationship with God. David didn't run, hide, or make excuses. He didn't pretend and he didn't minimize his mistakes. He accepted the worst about himself and openly surrendered his shortcomings to God right along with his successes. David, as he admitted his problems, used his failures as a lens through which he could get a better view of God's forgiveness. As he did this, his failures became building blocks of growth and maturity. Knowing that God was a gracious and forgiving God enabled David to repent and find ever greater joy and health in life. David knew that there are no sins that are too big for God to forgive. He also knew that God was not impressed with his success and that, as he responsibly faced his failures, God would not condemn him.

God knows us in an intimate way just like He knew David in an intimate way. Like it or not, we are all naked before Him. As we acknowledge this, God's love and power will heal our addictions and save our lives— just like He did for David, failures and all.

For you see, God understands when we feel conflicted. And He knows that we live in a conflicted world, too. He is aware that we are not happy with ourselves much of the time. Because He understands this, He never holds our struggles and conflicts against us.

He sees that our intentions are good most of the time. But He also sees that we run into problems when we try to control things that are beyond our ability to control. It hurts Him when He sees how we create problems for ourselves and other people because we don't ask for His help. But then, because He is compassionate, God knows that there is a reason for everything we do, a reason that that we usually don't know. When our addictions corrupt our motives, He knows it. He also knows that our motives are purified as we get honest. Feeling what we feel, He never loses sight of the fact that we pay a price when we get honest. Nevertheless, He is always urging us to move deeper into honesty because He knows that the price that we pay for dishonesty is far greater.

In Jesus, God assures us there are no sins that He is not willing to forgive and that there are no addictions that cannot be healed. With this in mind, He wants us to recognize in a deep way that the desire of our heart and the direction of our lives go hand in hand. He has created a world where we always have a choice in who we will become and what our lives will be like from here on out. So, He holds us responsible for our lives. For you see, it is the subtle and intimate decisions we make that will most profoundly impact our character and our lives. No matter what other people may say, God never laughs at us when we tell Him our plans. He never laughs at us, at all, in any way. God takes us more seriously than that. After all, He died so that we can have this opportunity to live.

God will, maybe, laugh when He sees how we try to make Him fit into the image that we make for Him. But then again, maybe not. After all, He knows that He is God and that we are not. Having expressed his love through Jesus, and having provided help for our addictions through people, God holds us fully responsible for our lives no matter what we say or think about Him. At the end of the day, He knows that we have no excuses.

God is the ultimate "more than." He is, in every way and at all times, more than we are and more than everything else, too. Only He can do for us what we cannot do for ourselves. With all of this in mind, it stands to reason that we will only know the intimate power of God once we have come to the end of our own resources and realize that we still need more. Having expressed himself in Christ, God is now willing to express himself in our lives as well. The only place for us to find life is in the life of Christ—God. This life of Jesus can never be contained in a history lesson or a theological discussion. He is more alive than that. He is to be lived in us! Jesus' life is now our life. His God is our God. Our lives are His. And now, we exist for God.

Everything will make sense for us when we are willing to look through the lens of eternity. The recovery that God gives is not about rule-keeping, religious moralizing, or self-imposed corrections. It is really the love of God that is changing our hearts and, as our hearts are changed, our minds will be changed, too. We are experiencing a complete change of personal allegiance, coming to prefer an intimate relationship with God above our addictions, above our lives, above everything.

Are you ready to say...

God, I surrender my will and my life to You today, this very moment, without reservation and with humble confidence, for You are my loving Father. Set me free from self-consciousness, from anxiety about tomorrow, and from the tyranny of the approval and disapproval of others, that I may find joy and delight simply and solely in pleasing You. May my inner freedom be a compelling sign of Your presence, Your peace, Your power, and Your love. Let Your plan for my life and the lives of all Your children gracefully unfold one day at a time. I love You with all my heart, and I place all my confidence in You, for You are my Abba Father.

    Attributed to Brennan Manning

Getting Intimate with God

"As he went out into the street, a man came running up, greeted him with great reverence, and asked, 'Good Teacher, what must I do to get eternal life?' Jesus said, 'Why are you calling me good? No one is good, only God. You know the commandments: Don't murder, don't commit adultery, don't steal, don't lie, don't cheat, honor your father and mother.' He said, 'Teacher, I have—from my youth—kept them all!' Jesus looked him hard in the eye—and loved him! He said, 'There's one thing left: Go sell whatever you own and give it to the poor. All your wealth will then be heavenly wealth. And come follow me.' The man's face clouded over. This was the last thing he expected to hear, and he walked off with a heavy heart. He was holding on tight to a lot of things, and not about to let go."

     Mark 10:17-22 *The Message*

"A saint is not someone who is good but someone who experiences the goodness of God."

     -Thomas Merton

We made a decision to turn our will and our lives over to the care of God as we understood him.

Scripture is full of people who can help us become more intimate with God. But it's not always because they had such a good relationship with God themselves. One such person is the man we read about in Mark 10. Let's call him Don. From what the Bible says, we know that Don rushes around in a big hurry, with all kinds of drama, all in an effort to do what he thinks he needs to do so that he can live forever. Sounds like some of us, doesn't it?

From what we read, we know that Don was intensely committed to his religious practice—rituals he had kept since childhood. Speculating a little, Don was probably the kind of guy who attended church without fail. We can almost see him, tall and well put-together. We can bet that Don took really good care of his appearance, presenting himself to the world with great care and consideration. He knew he was doing good and it was important to him to impress others with just how good he was. He probably drove a nice car and, secretly of course, he was proud that he kept his car looking and running better than anyone else in his neighborhood. For sure, Don was well respected at church and at home. This made him feel important. Being the man that he was, Don was obsessed with learning all that he needed to know in order to get rid of anything that limited the life that he loved so much. It seems like Don thought of Jesus as little more than a means to an end. Because Don was committed to getting everything that he thought was important, he inadvertently treated Jesus as if Jesus was just an object that was there to give Don what he thought he needed. Don was in control, or so he thought. In the most subtle of ways, Don was playing God. This is what we do when try to use God to get our way. It happens even with our best intentions. None of us means to objectify God but we do, at least to some degree. It's really not a question of if we have, but how often we have.

Jesus gave Don an amazing comeback. He didn't directly confront Don's religiosity and pride. He just suggested that Don should keep doing more of what he was already doing. Then, being such a hard worker and all, Don was apparently overcome with a deep, deep sadness. After all, since childhood he had been working harder and harder to get a better life and it obviously hadn't been working for him. If it had, he wouldn't have been so desperate for something more. So, deep in his gut, he knew it wasn't going to work now. Do you know this feeling?

Here the story could have taken a great turn, but it didn't. Jesus continued to respond to Don by challenging his attachments. (Don probably had some addictions mixed in there, too.) While challenging Don to detach and free himself from the things that he held so dear, Jesus extended an invitation to enter into the intimacy of living with Jesus on a day-to-day basis just like the rest of Jesus' followers did. Sadly, Don could not make this decision. He could not find it within himself to let go of the old life of religion and take hold of this new life of relationship.

We need to be careful not to speculate too much because we can't read Don's mind. We can only know for sure what Scripture tells us. Perhaps Don just didn't believe what Jesus was saying. Perhaps he couldn't fathom the idea that gaining eternal life did not depend on him alone. Or perhaps Don just didn't really want what Jesus had to offer. Don seemed determined to think that his religious discipline and control would be enough to get himself right with God forever. He chose pride over life.

Don's story will only benefit us if we are willing to learn from it. Sometimes we learn the most in observing the failures of others. It is important for us to relate ourselves to Don and his encounter with Christ, failures and all. For you see, Jesus is about more than just overcoming an addiction. He is about more than just going to heaven when we die. Any reason and all reasons are good reasons to come to Christ, but the only way we will continuously bring life to our sinful existence is to seek intimacy with Christ for the sake of God himself. Any other reason becomes sin sooner or later. Jesus is more than a religious icon. Jesus is how God identifies himself to us in a personal way. In Jesus, God shows himself as the perfect human so that all of us imperfect humans can enjoy a perfected relationship with God. It's simple really. As we make the decision to surrender our will and our life to Jesus, we get close, we get real and we get intimate with God. It's a love story, not a religious story. God looks deep into us and no matter what He sees, He loves us just like Jesus loved Don. What Jesus did for Don, God is doing for us. He challenges us. He calls us. He invites us to let go of the things which have been holding us back, most notably our religious attempts to prove ourselves worthy. God frees us from the demand that we get our act together. He knows that even if we did ever get our act together, all that we would ever have would be an act.

Christ is here to give us His life if we are willing to surrender the lifelessness that we have known up to now.

Step Four

We made a searching and fearless moral inventory of ourselves.

Steps One, Two and Three are discoveries and decisions that will help mold the future of our lives. Some people have reached basic sobriety as a result of these first three steps but, then again, some have not. Just because we may have stopped acting out in our addiction(s) does not mean we are recovering from them. Recovery needs action, and Step Four is about taking action.

Step Four is difficult. It can be frightening. But, we will find courage like we've never known before when we admit our fear, and then move forward anyway. For you see, courage never exists in the absence of fear. It's only when we feel fear that we can learn what it means to act with courage. Courage means to move forward in spite of fear—to move in the very direction in which we are afraid. We've already done this to some degree. It was, after all, somewhat scary when we turned our will and our life over to God. But we did it anyway. The desire to recover from our addictions compelled us. When we turned over our lives, we became a partner with God, partnering to develop His life in us. Step Four is part of our responsibility as a partner in the new life that God is giving to us. This is because God will not do for us what only we can do for ourselves.

We should use a notebook to record our memories, our thoughts and our feelings as we work through Step Four. Doing one section each day, let us always remember that those who avoid doing Step Four may not recover from their addictions.

Getting a Clear View

"God is in charge of human life, watching and examining us from the inside and out."

Proverbs 20:27 *The Message*

"It is not your diligence; it is not your examination of yourself that will enlighten you concerning sin. Instead, it is God who does all the revealing... If you try to be the one who does the examining, there is a very good chance that you will deceive yourself."

-Jeanne Guyon

We made a searching and fearless moral inventory of ourselves.

Every form of addiction is unique in that it has its own challenges and difficulties that must be addressed. On the other hand, every form of addiction will share some things in common with other addictions, too. For you see, addiction is really just one disease. It just happens to show itself in many, many different ways.

Those who suffer from one form of addiction can often relate very closely to those who suffer from other forms of addiction. Here are some examples:

- Alcoholics can understand the pain of withdrawal that many drug addicts experience when they attempt to stop using drugs.
- Someone who is obese because of an addiction to food can relate to the shame and self-hatred that many anorexics or bulimics feel.
- A man or woman who has been addicted to gambling knows quite well the obsession, and the pain, that a man or woman who is addicted to sex or pornography feels.

The common ground we share will amaze us, when we are willing to see it. Also, when we are willing, God can use our addictions to teach us compassion for others. Because, you see, our addictions have less to do with what we do, than why we do it. What is it that we experience that keeps us doing the destructive things we do? When we are willing to see the full spectrum of our addictions, we will see why addiction is sometimes called the most human of all diseases. We all have it, to some degree.

Addictions are about escape. When we act out, we are attempting to avoid uncomfortable feelings like fear, hopelessness, loneliness or the feeling of being unloved. We often have worked so hard to avoid our feelings that we have lost connection with what is really going on inside of us. Here is a simple fact that we must accept in order to recover from our addictions—we must face the truth about how we feel and how we have lived our lives. Our job in Step Four is to cultivate an increasing self-clarity of who we are, what we are about, why we think the way we do and why we do the things we do. If we want to recover from *all* of our addictions, the place to start is with the truth and the reality about *all* our lives. It is important that we understand that God is the God of truth. He is the God of reality. If we procrastinate or try to avoid the truth, we will, in effect, be trying to avoid God. And no one can do that for long.

Addictions are often a mosaic. When we act out in one way it often leads to acting out in other ways, too. To recover, we must accept the truth regarding *all* of our addictions. As we work through the following questions, let's try to see the big picture. Honesty, openness and willingness are required.

Questions to Consider

- What are the things that you do that are causing trouble for you and for other people?
- What is the primary addiction from which you need to recover?

- How old were you when you began the behaviors that turned into your addictions? Explain.
- How have your addictive behaviors increased over time?
- In what ways have you violated your own ethical standards as a result of your addictive behaviors?
- Do you do things when you are alone that you would not do if you were with others? What are they? Explain.
- List your addictions and write about how they have caused you financial difficulty.
- How have you abused yourself with unhealthy eating habits?
- Have you ever been dishonest with a medical professional in order to get prescriptions that were not necessary?
- How has your career suffered as a result of your addictions?
- How and why have you lied to others about your use of time?
- How and why have you lied to others about your use of money?
- In what ways have you misused family resources for your addictions?
- In what ways have you neglected yourself physically, emotionally or spiritually because of your addictions?
- What are you putting off regarding your inventory?

Recovering a Healthy Relationship with Ourselves

"But you desire honesty from the heart, so you can teach me to be wise in my inmost being."
>   Psalm 51:6 *NLT*

"The moral inventory is a cool examination of the damages that occurred to us during life and a sincere effort to look at them in true perspective. This has the effect of taking the ground glass out of us, the emotional substance that still cuts and inhibits."
>   - Bill Wilson

We made a searching and fearless moral inventory of ourselves.

No matter how we may rationalize it differently, our addictions have been destroying us. Part of the insanity of addiction is how we tend to minimize the damage that our addictions do. To whatever degree that we have brought pain into the lives of other people, we must admit it. But it is likely that we are the ones who have been hurt the most by our addictions.

This section of Step Four is an attempt to see how our addictions have hurt us individually. It is important that we be as objective as possible. We are not the focus. What we are looking to do is to recognize the causes and the conditions, the thinking and believing that have promoted the growth of addiction in our lives. We look ourselves over much like we would examine a part of our body that is hurting. We do it with care, in a nurturing way. Friendly, respectful, objective detachment is one way to look at it. We don't want to deny how we feel at any moment in time but, at the same time, this is not a sentimental journey, either.

We sift through our life, past and present, in order to identify the selfish thinking, the corrupted beliefs and the ineffective emotional maladjustments that promote our addictions. We need to understand that addictions grow because of self-centeredness. Addiction is not the cause of moral failings nor is it a moral failing in and of itself. Addiction and its subsequent moral failings are caused by spiritual and emotional longings that have gone unmet. Because of this, it is critical that we see how we have contributed to our own spiritual and emotional deprivation. For you see, our addictions take hold of us as we seek to meet needs that we cannot meet and escape pain that is too much for us to handle on our own. Sadly, in addiction, the very things that we have used to escape our pain actually increase our pain. Then, addictions grow and deepen all the more.

Most certainly, some of the pain we have experienced in life has come from other people. For now, let's just do our best to take a non-emotional look at what these people did to us and how it made us feel. For the sake of our recovery, it's important that we don't judge other people's motives. That is God's job, after all. He is the only One who has all the facts. We should just look at *what* they did, not *why* they did it. Let them work out their own troubles with God, just like we are doing. Any resentments that we have against others should be listed and cataloged. We will discuss them later, at the appropriate time and place.

As we move forward, God will give us courage. We will see things with a better focus. We may not be all that we thought we were. And that's okay. Whatever we are, God says that He loves us. In time we will grow to love ourselves, too.

Getting Clearer Perceptions

- Describe how you feel about yourself right after you have acted out in one of your addictions.

- How has your addiction affected the way you think about your life and your future?
- Describe the pain you feel when you consider the relationships you have lost because of your addictions.
- How have you objectified yourself financially, sexually or emotionally?
- Do you remember your first sexual experience? What was it?
- How have you violated your own sexual ethics?
- How have you been a hypocrite religiously, sexually or socially?
- Why and how do you feel sorry for yourself?
- How have you manipulated yourself with self-pity?
- Are you mad at yourself? Why?
- How have your addictions affected the goals and plans that you had for your life?
- Why would you sacrifice long-term health for short-term gratification?
- Do you work too much? Why?
- How have you exaggerated your successes?
- Have you ever asked yourself why you would ever do certain things?
- In what ways have you repeated dangerous experiences?
- How and why have you minimized your addictions and your mistakes?
- What are you avoiding?
- Do you like yourself? Why not?

Who's to Blame?

"People may be pure in their own eyes, but the LORD examines their motives."

Proverbs 16:2 *NLT*

"Whatever games are played with us, we must play no games with ourselves, but deal in our privacy with the last honesty and truth."

-Ralph Waldo Emerson

We made a searching and fearless moral inventory of ourselves.

Life is hard. Troubles come at us from every direction. Sometimes our troubles appear to be so big that it feels as if life itself is conspiring against us, keeping us from succeeding in the most important areas of our lives.

Perhaps more than most, people who struggle with addiction know what it's like to feel as if God and the whole world are against them. Sometimes we can even get a strange and sick kind of satisfaction from feeling this way. Succumbing to self-pity is an unhealthy way of trying to escape the reality of how we have lived irresponsibly. This is because when we are under the influence of self-pity, we alter the way we feel, all in a delusional attempt to sidestep the deep interpersonal convictions of truth that we do not want to face. Usually we won't directly tell others about the perceived injustices that we think that God—and life— have imposed on us. It's more likely that we'll just go through our days with a negative disposition, politely mentioning the undeserved troubles that we have. It is common to blame God for things that are not His fault, and as part of our Step Four inventory, we need to understand how we have blamed God for our troubles in the past. We need to get honest about this. Everyone blames God for something, and we certainly are no exception.

We know that God is all-powerful, but at the same time it is critical that we understand that He is not all-controlling. God creates people, not robots. He creates us with the dignity and the ability to make choices. Then the choices that we make impact our life and the lives of others. The effects of some choices will be good and others will be not so good. The choices that people make—and the results of those choices—are not God's responsibility. The relevant question for us is this: How can we cooperate with God in such a way that the bad things that have happened to us in the past can become things that are good for us today and in the future? For you see, in the past we have been our own worst enemy. In using self-pity and self-delusion, we have conspired against ourselves. In the past we would rather blame someone else for our troubles than to change ourselves and the way we live. We've hurt ourselves in ways that no one else could ever do. Remember, after all, that addiction is a self-assault.

Seeing things from God's point of view, we'll begin to recognize that God's plan for our lives is a kind of conspiracy, too. It is the conspiracy of grace and love. Scripture reveals how God has planned and intended—conspired, that is—to bring all people into a relationship with Him. This is the greatest conspiracy of all time, and the only one that will succeed forever. It is ongoing. No one can stop it or defeat it. In the end, no one will doubt that God's love will rule. For us, the only thing to doubt is whether we are ready and willing to act in a manner that will help us experience God's love in the here and now.

As we work through this section of questions, let's look at how we have inhibited God's love in our lives. We all have blamed God for things that were not His fault. He knows it and He is not holding it against us today. This is our chance to get in better touch with our inner reality and, in so doing, we'll get in touch with God in a more honest and realistic way.

Let's Get Real

- What difficulties do you have that cause you to blame God?
- How have you expressed unwarranted pride and anger when people and the world did not cooperate with your plans?
- How have you tried to manipulate your feelings through self-pity?
- How and when and with whom do you feel excluded and deprived?
- When did you first think that you may have an addiction?
- Who hurt you? Was it parents, other family members, people from church or school, neighbor, enemy, friend?
- How have you blamed God for the hurt that others have done to you?
- How have you violated or objectified others sexually, personally or socially?
- How have you defied your spiritual convictions as a result of your addictions?
- Who is the target of your jealousy and why?
- How have you been greedy?
- How has your addiction affected your relationship with God?
- How have you been determined to get your own way?
- How have you confused God with church?
- How have you confused religious activity with an intimate relationship with God?
- When and why do you feel self-pity?
- What do you feel guilty about?
- Why do you lie?

Truth in Relationship

"Make a careful exploration of who you are and the work you have been given, and then sink yourself into that. Don't be impressed with yourself. Don't compare yourself with others. Each of you must take responsibility for doing the creative best you can with your own life."
      Galatians 6:4,5 *The Message*

"Honesty is the first chapter of the book of wisdom."
      -Thomas Jefferson

We made a searching and fearless moral inventory of ourselves.

The people around us get hurt by our addictions. But in recovery we can benefit the lives of others, too. Step Four is as much about people as it is about addiction. What we do in Step Four is personal, both to us and to others. This is because of the personal nature of our relationships. Relationships are personally organic because people are organic. We all impact the lives of others. We can't help it; it's the way we are. People are both blessed and cursed by one another.

Next to God, our relationships with other people are the greatest influences in our lives. This doesn't mean that everything will be great all of the time. When we look at other people in a realistic way, we'll see that they are tremendous sinners. And we'll see that they look a whole lot like us because we are tremendous sinners, too. Above all of this, what becomes amazingly clear is a subtle yet profound goodness in each of us. As we come to grips with our profound sinfulness—and the fact that God loves us anyway—we are able to recognize a God-given dignity and worth inside of all people. We'll recognize that no one can really be defined in terms of good versus bad. We all have an original worthiness that is completely human, as shown through our obvious flaws and shortcomings, and more than human at the same time. Instinctively, it seems, we all want more out of life than what we can provide for ourselves. We fall short. We are sinners who are reaching out for something that we cannot get on our own.

Step Four is not about making judgments. It is about getting an honest awareness of who we are and how we have lived. We want to see how we have damaged our relationships with other people. Working through Step Four will help us learn to live in such a way that we won't be so easily influenced to do things that hurt us or others. God is our strength. He is working to build us up according to His will. So we don't need to worry about what other people say or think about us. It's not like we have any control over them anyway. We just live our lives with God, honestly. We let God take care of others. We don't need to feel pity for them, or for ourselves. However, we do need to develop a keen awareness of how we have allowed others to influence us in the past, sometimes for good and other times not so good.

We can approach our personal and moral inventories in different ways, but there will probably be some common characteristics. We bring our willingness to the table and we face some tough questions about how our attitude and our behavior have affected those around us. Then we write down what comes to mind. We write down everything about our families that we think is important. We write down every thought, every memory and every feeling, the best we can. We write about the people who have harmed us and we write about the people who we have harmed. We write a great deal about our sexual experiences as well as any experiences that we have had with drugs, alcohol, money, gambling, food and/or anything else that has been a problem for us at any time in our lives. We write about why we did the things we did. We write about how we felt when we were doing them, and how we felt after we did them. We write about love, what we desired for love to be like and how we have been disappointed by those we loved. We write it all. We write everything.

Questions That Need to Be Answered

- How have you disregarded or abused those weaker than you?
- Who were the people that you hurt in this way?
- How have you envied the talents and resources other people had that you did not have?
- How has your addiction affected your relationship with your religious family?
- How have you been selfish?
- What makes you feel entitled to do things that you know are wrong?
- How have you valued your addiction more than your spouse and your children?
- How have your family, your employer or others been hurt by your moral failings or your insensitivities?
- What are some of the things that others have been denied because you were absorbed in your addiction?
- What are some specific ways that you have exhibited selfishness?
- How have you been careless with your spouse, your children, your employer and your neighbors?
- In what ways have you put your own needs and interests above the needs and interests of others?
- How and why have you lied to your loved ones?
- How has your employer been hurt by your addictions?
- When and with whom do you feel self-pity?
- What do you feel guilty about?
- What do you like about yourself?
- Why do you lie?

Seeing the Big Picture

"... First! Wash the inside of the cup, and then the outside will become clean, too."
     Matthew 23:26 *NLT*

"I am not good, only God is good. However, as I get to know God better, I am being made better."
     Anonymous

We made a searching and fearless moral inventory of ourselves.

It is vitally important that we recognize all of the ways that addiction has become part of our lives. Tragically, many people begin their recovery journey only to become derailed by other addictions that they didn't recognize and address. Addiction—most often thought of as related to alcohol, food, drugs, sex, and gambling—is more accurately thought of as any kind of destructive dependency. Addiction is almost limitless in the way that it can destroy our lives.

Today it is becoming ever more common for treatment centers to diagnose their patients with co-occurring addictions that parallel and commingle with the originally identified addiction. For the sake of our recovery, it is important for us to evaluate all aspects of our addictions(s), the best we can. If we don't, our most pronounced addiction cannot be healed.

The list of common addictions includes:

- Mind and mood-altering substances like alcohol, nicotine and other drugs
- A burdening need to work, achieve or succeed
- Overspending, gambling, or hoarding money

- An unhealthy view of sex, craving pornography and/or romantic relationships
- Approval seeking and having unhealthy dependencies on family and other people
- Unbalanced desire for exercise, the need to look good or pursuing unnecessary medical procedures
- Addictions related to food and/or the aversion to food
- Unhealthy view of religion, and/or over emphasis on religious practice that reduces the intimacy of personal spirituality

Honestly addressing all of our addictions helps us become more open to God. Exercising the humility to recognize and admit our most subtle addictions enables us to experience courage like we have never experienced it before. In this way, God will make it possible for *all* of our addictions to be transformed into healthy and powerful assets. With this in mind, let us not blind ourselves to any of our addictions. Whatever addiction we ignore can potentially reignite our most powerful addictions, bringing great harm to our lives and to the lives of our loved ones.

Things to Think About

- How would you describe your most profound addiction?
- Write down some of the various ways that you have been triggered to act out in your primary addiction.
- What are some of the social environments that tempt you to act out?
- Who are some of the people who tempt you to act out?
- What are some of the things that you do under the influence of your addiction that you would not otherwise do?
- What foods do you crave when you are sad, lonely or tired?
- Name some things that you have done while acting out that you had previously thought you would never do.
- When you think about your addiction, what are some of the other things you crave that you know are not right for you?

- How have you "accidentally" found yourself acting out in your addiction when you just meant to have some fun in another way?

Inner Reality

"Let's take a good look at the way we're living and reorder our lives under God."
Lamentations 3:40 *The Message*

"If we want to know God personally, the place to start is with the truth and reality about ourselves."
-Anonymous

We made a searching and fearless moral inventory of ourselves.

Being real about our emotions is one of the healthiest commitments we can make. When we deny our feelings, we deny the reality of our innermost lives; we reject a fundamental aspect of our own humanity. We reduce ourselves. We become objects in our own eyes. We lose the very dignity that we most desire.

Nicole was a wonderful young woman whose life had become paralyzed because she could not honestly address her feelings. Along with the rest of her family, Nicole suffered because of her father's domineering abusiveness, an abusiveness that he called religious leadership. As a little girl, Nicole often felt hurt because her mother and father ignored her attempts to gain their affection. Her parents, mostly her father, were so absorbed in their own lives that they didn't care for Nicole in the way that a little girl of her age needed to be nurtured. Because of this, Nicole grew up feeling unwanted. No matter how hard she tried, she was never able to connect with her father in a way that made her feel loved by him. He had a problem himself. He could not connect with his own feelings, let alone with the feelings of his little girl. Nicole feared that she would never get her father's love. By adolescence, Nicole was angry. By college, she had a deep resentment toward her mother, her brothers and sisters, church, God and—most of all—herself. Blind to her own feelings, Nicole continued to love her father and, with a desperate heart, she held out hope that someday he would love her, too.

The greatest tragedy of Nicole's story is how she began to self-destruct in her own addictions even while she maintained all the appearances of a successful businesswoman. Because she was unable to recognize and admit how she really felt on the inside, it was impossible for her to get the help she needed. Nicole fell into a pattern of dangerous addictions and ultimately she died at the age of 34 from complications related to alcoholism and anorexia. Nicole died believing that she was at fault and that her mother, brothers, sisters and God had all conspired together to keep her father's love from her. She never recognized the fear and abandonment that she felt. Nor did she admit the justifiable anger she felt for her father. The last words she heard him say to her were words of criticism because of her drinking and her emaciated appearance. But still, even with her deep wounds, she idolized him till she died. She never could see that he was the one who was wrong. Nor could she admit that she was mad at him for the way he treated her. Nicole's life and death prove that unacknowledged fear, anger and resentment can be fatal.

Identifying, recognizing and admitting how we feel is a commitment to intimate truth. If we want to be healed, we must first be known. Being known starts with knowing how we feel about ourselves, our lives, other people and God. We are responsible for knowing how we feel. If we don't know how we feel, we will carry our pain and fears with us into the future. Denying fear actually makes us full of fear. Fear—like anger, resentment and all other painful emotions—swells up inside of us when it goes unaddressed, setting us up in a sort of psychic paralysis from which we cannot save ourselves. We get stuck; we are alone. This kind of isolation is perhaps the worst of human suffering, and nothing will free us from our emotional isolation unless we get real about how we feel. We have to have help. Failing to admit what we feel and failing to get the help we need is what killed Nicole. So, to ensure that we don't suffer the same fate that Nicole suffered, we get real as we work our Step

Four. The purpose of Step Four is to help us recognize specific thoughts and feelings that we have that are not effectively working for us. If we are going to make effective changes, we have to know what needs to be changed. Human as we are, we are going to feel fear from time to time. We are going to get mad and we will become resentful sometimes, too. Having these feelings is not a problem. Denying them and avoiding them is. So, in order to get healthier we must get real like never before. We must exercise courage in Step Four. Just because we feel fear doesn't mean we can't act with courage. In fact, courage never exists in the absence of fear. It's more like courage and fear are two sides of the same coin of emotion. To find courage, we must first acknowledge our fear. Then, we take our fear and we turn it over. We admit it and we give it up to God just like we gave our addictions to Him. When we turn over our fear to God and become ready to take action, He will empower us to act with courage even when we still feel afraid. The courage that God gives helps us to know the reality of our inner life in a powerfully intimate way. With the courage that God gives, we can take the most personal areas of our lives and give ourselves away in empathy to others. In this way we can touch the very souls of those who are closest to us, passing along the courageous life that we are discovering, helping others to discover it, too. Doing this makes our lives all worthwhile.

As you read through and answer the following questions, take a few minutes and pray that God will help you to understand how to make the pain of your past a blessing to others in the future.

Look Inside

- What have you done in the past that most troubles you today?
- Name and write about the person or persons that make you feel angry, hurt or afraid when you think about them.
- Can you identify how some of your anger at yourself or others has promoted your addictive behavior? How?
- What do you fear most?

- How do you feel about those who are stronger than you?
- How do you feel about those in authority over you?
- Are you mad at any members of your family? Why?
- How do you punish yourself for mistakes you made in the past?
- What habits do you have that are destructive to your body?
- What habits do you have that are destructive to your relationships?
- What habits do you have that are destructive to your finances?

All Things Good

"The time is coming when everything will be revealed; all that is secret will be made public."
    Luke 12:2 *NLT*

"To state the facts frankly is not to despair for the future nor indict the past."
    - John F. Kennedy

We made a searching and fearless moral inventory of ourselves.

Jesus Christ is *the* definitive break in what has previously been an unbreakable cycle of human effort, human trial and human failure. And this cycle has been repeated in every human life throughout history. But no more. Through Christ, God changes all the rules. In Christ, the new rule is human trial, human failure, and redemption for every man and woman who trusts in the redemptive love of God. It's very simple, really. God, through Christ, has done for us what we could never do for ourselves. So, we no longer need to be concerned with getting ourselves right with God. We need only concern ourselves with honestly addressing the reality of our addictions and our sins. It is vitally important that we understand our shortcomings with as much clarity as possible, because we can only accept God's love to the degree that we accept our personal shortcomings. God will do for us what we cannot do for ourselves, but He will *not* do for us what only we can do for ourselves.

Looking back over our lives, we will inevitably see that we have made some bad choices along the way. Seeing things from an objective point of view, we can see that the choices that we made, even the bad ones, usually made sense to us at the time that we made them. Being objective in this way, we can give ourselves compassion and understanding, which will help us to move forward and live our lives with more freedom. We don't need to judge ourselves anymore. Judgment is God's job, after all, not ours. For our part, we just let the facts be what they are. God makes perfectly enlightened judgments about the things we do and why we do them. For you see, God does not judge us solely on what we do. He does not define us by our actions alone. He defines us by the love that He has for us. He knows that we don't know all that we need to know. He knows that we are not always in control of ourselves. He knows that we are instinctively fearful and self-centered and that sometimes we do bad things with good intentions, and that other times we do things that look good on the outside but are done with selfish motives. Knowing all things, and with His perfect judgment, God does not define us in terms of good versus bad. Having created us as very complex creatures, God is fully aware, as proven through Christ's compassion, that we live conflicted lives in a conflicted world. From God's point of view, we are defined by the simple reality of His revolutionary love for lost and addicted sinners like us.

Because of Christ, it is no longer necessary for us to avoid or escape the pain that we experience in life. In Christ, we can find a good purpose in everything. In faith, we believe that He makes all things good. And because there is no limitation to the meaning of "all," we can accept every pain and difficulty as an opportunity for goodness. Pain can be a great teacher and a wonderful motivator. Pain compels us forward, motivating us to reach out. It's as if our past problems, fears, pains and sins become monuments along the road of our journey. They become memorable points of progress that help us—and others, too—to journey deeper into the empowering love of God.

We want to be as thorough as we can possibly be, but—at the same time— we want to recognize that our faith is in God and not in our own efforts. When we feel anger, we write about it. When we sense fear, we write about it. When we feel resentment, we write it down. We write everything down so that we can talk it over face-to-face with God, and man-to-man with another person, too. We don't need to be perfect, but we do want to do the best that we can. As we get a better grasp about how we feel, we will get a better grasp of who we are and how we have harmed ourselves and others. Then, we become increasingly ready to change. We become ready to live in this world in a new and better way.

Write down all that you think needs to be written down.

Step Five

Admitted to God, to ourselves and to another human being the exact nature of our wrongs.

Step Five is one of the most difficult things that we will do in our recovery. It is also one of the most rewarding, too. While our addictions have created relational barriers, Step Five will help us cultivate healthier relationships with God and the people that He brings into our lives.

In Step Five, we'll share all of the things that we uncovered about ourselves when we made our Step Four inventory. We'll take what we have learned about ourselves and we'll lay it all out on the table, and talk it over with God and another person. We won't hide or change anything. We'll just let God— and someone else—see things for what they are, and we'll let them see us for who we are, too. We will share what our lives have been like as well as what we are like, both the good and the bad. We have no reason to run, hide or make excuses. We'll acknowledge that we've created many of the problems that we face. And, at the same time, we will acknowledge that we are responsible for all of the problems that we face, even the ones that we didn't create. For many of us this will be the first time in our lives that the honest reality of our lives will be received with respect and appreciation.

Moving forward, in Step Five, we have the chance to become healthier, happier and better integrated members of the majestic world God has created for us to live in. Let's make the most of this opportunity.

Admitting to God

"He who conceals his sins does not prosper, but whoever confesses and renounces them finds mercy. Blessed is the man who always fears the LORD, but he who hardens his heart falls into trouble."
Proverbs 28:13-14 *NLT*

"My false and private self is the one who wants to exist outside the reach of God's will and God's love – outside of reality and outside of life. And such a self cannot help but be an illusion."
- Thomas Merton

Admitted to God, to ourselves and to another human being the exact nature of our wrongs.

Getting honest about the details of our lives is the most powerful thing we can do to strengthen our intimate connection with God. Honesty puts us on the same page with Him. Knowing that He knows everything about us, there is no reason to hide what is inside of us anymore. When we get honest with God, we "cash the check" so to speak; we open ourselves up and receive the grace that He has already provided for us through Christ.

Step Five is not a religious exercise, so it's important that we don't over-spiritualize this aspect of our recovery. We are just admitting, with as much detail as we can, what God already knows. We acknowledge that we have never benefited from minimizing our weaknesses and shortcomings. We admit our pride and our stubbornness, with as much clarity as possible, most notably all of our silly attempts to solve our spiritual and emotional problems. We confess that we have been self-righteous in covert and creative ways. We admit that we have never fooled God and that we rarely fooled anyone else, only ourselves. We tell the details about how we have judged other people and, with as much humility as possible, we admit how our religiosity has kept God—and the goodness that He intends for us—at arm's length.

God has known us in a deep way. Now we will begin to know ourselves in a deep way, too. As we are willing to admit the exact nature of our wrongs to God, we will be able to embrace the acceptance that He gives and then begin to accept ourselves in the same way—even the worst about us. The more we admit our shortcomings to God, the more we slice away at the fears that have ruled us from the inside. We will learn to be at peace with the mysterious ways of God. Embracing His deep acceptance, we will no longer be obsessed with trying to figure out the hidden streams and currents of God. We will lose our inhibitions. We will want to strip down, reveal ourselves completely and swim in the power of goodness that God offers to us. We will never sink or get lost when we are honest with God. He'll do the navigating for us. Realizing that we are known by God in this intimate way, we can live at rest. We will be buoyed in His grace forever, floating and moving with the currents of His guidance and care. There is no need to fear the oceanic mystery of God anymore. No matter where His currents lead our lives, the ultimate destination for us is more than very, very good.

Jerry Gets Honest with Himself

"You're blessed when you're content with just who you are – no more, no less. That's the moment you find yourselves proud owners of everything that can't be bought."

Matthew 5:5 *The Message*

"The heart is the deepest essence of a person. It symbolizes what's at our core. The heart of the matter is that we can know and be known only through revealing what's in our heart."

-Brennan Manning

Admitted to God, to ourselves and to another human being the exact nature of our wrongs.

Hello, my name is Jerry and I am an alcoholic. I was 51 years old when I first said these words and I've been saying them almost every day for the past three-and-a-half years. I started drinking when I was in college. Getting drunk with my fraternity brothers was a lot of fun. Unfortunately, unlike most of my friends, I never stopped. Near the end of my drinking, I was actually drinking less often. Not because I wanted to drink any less but because I knew in my heart of hearts that my drinking was hurting my family and me. I never meant to hurt anyone.

I had gotten married at 25, and by 31 I had three beautiful daughters, a solid marriage (it looked like it on the outside), a great career and I was a leader in my church. While near the end of my drinking I was consuming less alcohol, the people around me were complaining about it more and more. They were pointing out problems that were happening because of my drinking. Even though I was drinking less, my drinking was affecting me more. Finally, the employee assistance director at work confronted me. He gave me the choice of going to a treatment program for alcoholism that the company would pay for, or the company would demote me to a less prestigious position. My ego refused the demotion so I chose rehab.

In rehab I was confronted by my wife and daughters about how my drinking and my attitude had been hurting them for years. I was dumbfounded. I had no idea how they felt. Also, the doctor at the rehab told me that I had suffered liver damage, and that I had what they called "level two alcoholism." I wasn't sure what that meant but it sure got my attention. I wasn't able to sleep and my body shook for days. I was nervous and uncomfortable for three weeks after my last drink. Worst of all, as my head cleared, I became more and more ashamed of how I had let the years slip by and how I had hurt my wife and daughters. I knew that I had always loved them, but I could not escape the reality of how I had held them hostage for so long. Being given the opportunity to recover, I knew that this is what I wanted to do. I wanted to change.

I started to attend Alcoholics Anonymous meetings while in rehab and I have never stopped. I go to an average of two to three meetings per week, depending on my schedule and my disposition. I got a sponsor and I began working the steps on a personal basis. I spent about a month working through my Step Four inventory. I worked on it every day. Finally I sat down with my sponsor and read much of what I had written down to him. I also told him a lot of things that came to mind as we were sitting there talking.

While doing Step Four, I learned a lot about myself. In a nutshell, I learned that my alcoholism was only a disease and not my real problem. My real problem was me, and I would continue to be my own worst problem until I admitted this to myself, just like I had to admit to myself that I was an alcoholic. If I were to ever become a better person, free from alcoholism *and* selfishness, I had to admit just how selfish I had been. Being intentional and committed to self-honesty was the only way that I could help myself overcome the deep-seated selfishness that had ruled me throughout my life.

In doing Step Four, I began to see what I needed to see in order to confront the self-deception that had hurt me and those around me, particularly my wife and children. As I admitted the exact nature of my personal wrongs to myself, I was able to feel my lifelong self-idolatry begin to fall away. It felt like God was helping me to set myself aside and make other people more important than me. In doing this, I surrendered 51 years of misguided assumptions that had made me think that I was invincible, entitled and important. My alcoholism proved to me that I had lived in a self-imposed delusion. I had been trying to rule myself, rule my family and rule my world, all in the name of being the "leader" in my home.

As I admitted these things to myself, I accepted myself at my worst for the first time in my life. As I accepted myself at my worst, I began to know grace as only God can give it. This new grace is more than just a subject I had heard about in church. It is a real world, here and now. It is an overpowering, and sometimes painful, movement toward honesty. I first noticed it when I sat alone in rehab, crying uncontrollably. That day, amidst the pain that I was experiencing, God's grace helped me to have a sense that things were going to change and that I would get the help that I had been too afraid to seek.

I know that I don't deserve the goodness that has taken hold of me. As I have become honest about my character shortcomings, I have been able to surrender a battle that I had been losing all of my life. The more explicit and honest I have been with myself, the more effective my repentance has been. And, I have found an energy that gives me the stamina to follow the path that God gives me to travel. Without an effective path to follow and the strength that God gives me to follow it, I could never truly repent or change. I thank God for my alcoholism and for my Twelve Step journey, specifically Step Five. Getting honest with myself and learning to accept myself as someone that God is willing to work with has been a turning point in my life. Letting go of my self denials has not only helped me to quit drinking, but helped me to become a new kind of man who now brings goodness and delight to his wife and his family.

Becoming Our Friend

"If we claim that we're free of sin, we're only fooling ourselves. A claim like that is errant nonsense. On the other hand, if we admit our sins – make a clean break of them – he won't let us down, he'll be true to himself. He'll forgive our sins and purge us of all wrongdoing. If we claim that we've never sinned, we out-and-out contradict God – make a liar out of him. A claim like that only shows off our ignorance of God."
   I John 1:8-10 *The Message*

"Tell the truth. It will confound your enemies and astound your friends."
   -Mark Twain

Admitted to God, to ourselves and to another human being the exact nature of our wrongs.

Jerry does a great job of telling us what it was like for him to get honest and admit what he was really thinking and feeling on the inside. As he became honest with himself, he was better able to get honest with God as well as those who were close to him. Jerry discovered that self-honesty was required for his good intentions to become reality. This simple principle holds true for all of us.

Trust is a by-product of honesty. It is essential for all healthy relationships, whether it's a relationship with someone else or our relationship with ourselves. We all have people in our lives that we don't trust because they have not been honest with us. When we can't trust someone, we can't feel at peace with them, comfortable with them or have a real friendship with them. It's the same way with ourselves. When we are dishonest with ourselves we won't feel comfortable, and we won't be able to be at peace with ourselves. This is why we so often resort to some kind of mood- or mind-altering experience. Knowing this helps us to better understand how our addictions have become entrenched inside of us. We will also better understand why we have felt lonely and isolated for so much of our lives.

In the past, we've seen ourselves through a lens of deception and secrets. Now, we throw off the blinders so that we can see ourselves more realistically. By admitting to ourselves the *truth* about ourselves, we become better integrated with the reality of life. The holes inside of us get plugged up and the bleeding stops. The broken pieces of our hearts and minds start to find their right places again. We become ready to receive God's compassion and care, which will take root in the very places where our personal deceptions have lived. This blows the lid off the box that our addictions have placed us in. Our identity—that we were made in the image of God—finds new life as we become connected with God in this way.

We become the most blessed of all people when we get honest with God and ourselves. We go from being our own worst enemy to being one of our most intimate friends. In purging the dishonesty from our lives, we purge the things that have been destroying us. And we see how our future will be good, irrespective of the difficulties that come our way. Our days will be brighter, the sun will be warmer, the breezes of life will be cooler and fresher. We will find life is worth living well.

Marie's Story

"Make this your common practice: Confess your sins to each other and pray for each other so that you can live together whole and healed."
James 5:16 *The Message*

"By getting real and being honest with others, we make ourselves available to be loved by them."
- An Anonymous Recovering Addict

Admitted to God, to ourselves and to another human being the exact nature of our wrongs.

I began my Twelve Step experience hoping to deal with my extreme worry over my two adult sons and their use of alcohol. I also have a grown daughter, but she has never done drugs and she doesn't drink. I drank and did a lot of drugs myself, when I was in high school and early college. I went to a large Catholic university, where I met my husband during my junior year. My partying slowed down when I met him, and it stopped once we graduated and got married. My husband drinks occasionally, but he never gets drunk. In fact, he doesn't like the "buzzed" feeling. I think my sons got the alcoholic gene from my side of the family. My dad and mom were both functional alcoholics and I think I would have become an alcoholic, too, if I hadn't quit drinking when I did.

My addiction is the way that I try to control the lives of my children, mainly my two boys. I am a control freak. As far back as I can remember, I have feared the worst for myself, my husband, and my children. I have feared that they would lose control of themselves and get hurt. I have feared that my family would suffer calamity and shame. I have feared that my two boys would grow up to be like my dad and my mom had been with their drinking.

My recovery started when I joined a women's support group at my church. The lady who ran this group was married to a recovering alcoholic. Her husband had been sober for years and she had been involved with Al-Anon for years herself. I loved her attitude and her cheerful strength. All of us in the group were attracted to her transparency and her confidence. Through her encouragement I began working the and attending Al-Anon meetings with her. I worked the Twelve Steps dutifully and I enjoyed the Al-Anon meetings very much, even though I felt embarrassed at the thought of others finding out about me going to Al-Anon. I've always feared that people would find out just how dysfunctional my family and I really were. I guess I should only speak this way about myself. My husband is a wonderful man, after all. I love him dearly and I so enjoy the time we spend together. My daughter is smart, lovely and strong-willed. My two sons, while I do worry about their drinking, are grown with successful careers and nice families. They both maintain their lives with dignity and responsibility. I guess I can say that I am proud of them, even though they are not all that I wanted them to be.

As I worked though my Step Four inventory, I realized that I had unknowingly been more committed to maintaining my own reputation within my community and my church than I was to benefiting my family. I learned that where I thought I was being a good mother and wife, I was actually being manipulative and selfish. Without realizing it, I was dominating my family, mainly my two sons, all in an attempt to get them to act and live the way I thought they should. Instead of helping them, I was hurting them. Instead of being a loving mother, like I thought I was, I was being a tyrant. Instead of letting them live their own lives, I was trying to get them to live the life that I was not able to live. I admit that most of my attempts to control the lives of my children had really never helped them; in fact, it hurt them. I admit that the anxiety I have felt for so long has been the result of me trying to control things that are beyond my ability to control—my two sons in particular. I admit that I have dumped my anxiety onto my family. It hurts to admit these things.

When it came time to talk it over with another person, I sat down with my sponsor—the lady who ran the support group at church—and I read to her all that I had learned about myself while doing my Step Four inventory. It took a couple of hours and she was very patient. We sat at an outdoor café in the afternoon. We had lunch and then we drank tea. We took breaks when we felt the need. When I had finally finished reading to her all that I had written down in my Step Four, she looked at me and she said, "Is that all?" Before I could say yes to her question, my mind jumped back to something that happened 30 years before, when I was a sophomore in college—something I had forgotten about. Immediately I felt a hot flush come to my face. I felt embarrassed and afraid because I had just remembered a secret that I knew that I needed to get off my chest. After a moment's pause, I spilled my guts. I told her about having a sexual experience with a female friend in my dorm. I knew that I was not a lesbian and I had never really been promiscuous. Other than my husband, I had only had sex with two other people, a boy I dated as a freshman and this other girl in my dorm. I don't know why I had forgotten about this for so many years, but I had. I don't know why I remembered it when I did, but once I remembered it, I knew that I needed to tell someone about it.

After I told my sponsor about this memory, she sat back in her chair, took a sip of her tea and then, looking me straight in the eye, told me that she had a similar experience that she kept secret until she did her Step Five with her sponsor. Hearing her tell me this made me feel like someone had just thrown cold water in my face. I was stunned. I know I imagined this, but I thought I heard the sound of glass breaking in the distance, as if someone had just broken through. It had never occurred to me that someone else may have done the same thing that I had done. I don't mean to imply that I am judgmental about other people's lives, but because I have always had deep moral convictions, I felt guilty about having this experience with this other girl. Having my sponsor share her experience helped me to better understand that we all make mistakes and that our past mistakes do not necessarily dictate who we are today. Health and happiness have less to do with our past than they have to do with letting go of our secrets. In my case, it was not the past that was troubling me, it was my secrets. They were my problem all along. In order for me to have the kind of life that I had always wanted, it was necessary for me to recognize and admit that I could not control my life by controlling the lives of others. And I needed to recognize and admit that my failures could be accepted by others if I would be willing to get honest about them. Admitting my shortcomings to myself and another person has released me from a burden that was silently killing me and hurting those I loved.

Getting honest has freed me in other areas of my life, too. I have come to understand that my co-dependency is selfish and that it works against my faith in God. I now see that my sinfulness is the result of me not trusting in God's power and love. My lack of faith has hurt me and it has hurt others. By learning to trust God in a more personal way, I can admit that my greatest fear was that I would be embarrassed and ashamed. Not because my family was bad—because they aren't—but because, co-dependently, I wanted everyone to think that I was so good. This is what was really hurting me all along.

My Step Five experience has done more for me than I ever anticipated it would. It's helped me to let go of my need to look perfect. I can be real now. My life is more relaxed because I am more relaxed. The little struggles I have don't get me down so much anymore. Before, while I didn't drink or smoke like I did in college, I always missed the drinking and smoking, and on occasion I would slip up. Mostly, I had stayed away from these things by willpower alone, but I missed them at the same time. Now that I have become more honest about who I really am on the inside, I hardly think about drinking and smoking at all. And when I do, they just don't appeal to me like they once did. I feel as though I have shed 50 pounds of excess baggage that I have been carrying around for as long as I can remember.

I am learning to be content with who I am. I am at peace. I thank God for my Step Five experience, for my wonderful sponsor and for my imperfectly delightful family.

Being the Real Deal

"Finally, I confessed all my sins to you and stopped trying to hide them. I said to myself, *I will confess my rebellion to the LORD.* And you forgave me! All my guilt is gone."
     Psalm 32:5

"We hide what we know or feel ourselves to be (which we assume to be unacceptable and unlovable) behind some kind of appearance which we hope will be more pleasing. We hide behind pretty faces which we put on for the benefit of our public. And in time we may even come to forget that we are hiding, and think that our assumed pretty faces is what we really look like."
     - Simon Tugwell

Admitted to God, to ourselves and to another human being the exact nature of our wrongs.

Honesty is the best investment that we can make in our recovery. No one can do this for us. We have to do it for ourselves. When we invest ourselves, honestly, it will always pay off for us in very, very good ways. We will discover an authentic goodness about ourselves that we never knew existed. We will find an inner confidence that is unlike anything we have ever known before.

Most of us, like our friend Marie, have gone through our lives attempting to solve problems that were not ours to solve. Focusing on other people's problems keeps us from facing the reality of our own lives. This kind of avoidance is what keeps us from experiencing the happy, joyous and free life that God has to give. Marie's growing honesty, while still in progress, gives us a wonderful picture of how we can, like Marie, make peace with ourselves by accepting the reality of our failures and shortcomings, and then openly and honestly sharing them with God and another person. By recognizing and admitting the painful reality of her splintered heart, Marie was able to find the quality of life and personal relationships that she had been searching for all of her life. This kind of openness and honesty transforms our perspectives. It changes how we think and feel about God, ourselves and other people. It breaks down the walls of isolation. Having the experience of being heard, observed, known, included, loved and embraced, in spite of our addictions, sins and mistakes, radically changes everything about us. When we receive the power of love that someone else gives to us through their listening ear, compassion and understanding soak into us deeply. The poison of self-hatred and condemnation get washed away.

Like Marie, we need to recognize and admit the ways that we have been trying to control our lives by manipulating others. We need to admit how we have been selfish, even when we have hidden it within religious practice or good appearances. The masks we wear will suffocate us. Without honest confession, we will begin to believe our own deceptions. We will begin to think that we really are the actors and pretenders that we have portrayed ourselves to be. On the other hand, getting honest with another person is the foundation of healthy, trusting relationships. If we don't do this, we will have no one to trust but ourselves, and become a prisoner of our own fear and deceit. We'll become all the more alone. Inevitably, we will become more foolish and less capable of making solid decisions for our lives. We will want relief from our pain, but we won't have it because we are unwilling to open ourselves up to God and get honest with others. To not be open and to not share ourselves honestly puts us in the horrible position of being our greatest abuser and our greatest victim, as well.

If we are not willing to share all that we are with God and another person, we will not move toward wholeness and integrity. Establishing a trusting relationship with God and another person creates an environment where spiritual and emotional wholeness will flourish inside of us. In Scripture, God says that we are all sinners and that we are all loved by Him. God also says that we can all be saved by the grace He showed us in the life of Jesus Christ. All that God requires of us is that we become honest about our sinful condition and honestly ask for His help.

If we think or claim anything more than this, be it good or bad, we will deceive ourselves. If we deceive ourselves, we will never enjoy the life that God has to give us. God gives real life to real people. If we want to have the real life that God has to give us, we will have to get real ourselves.

Taking the Next Step

"Now that we know what we have—Jesus, this great High Priest with ready access to God—let's not let it slip through our fingers. We don't have a priest who is out of touch with our reality. He's been through weakness and testing, experienced it all—all but the sin. So let's walk right up to him and get what he is so ready to give. Take the mercy, accept the help."

> Hebrews 4:14-16 *The Message*

"Nothing makes us so lonely as our secrets."
> - Paul Tournier

Admitted to God, to ourselves and to another human being the exact nature of our wrongs.

With whom are we going to get real? To whom will we get honest and make our admissions? Some general guidelines will help us find the right kind of person, who will help us make the most of our Step Five experience. It is important for us to understand first and foremost that there is no one particular person who can completely accept us—and all that we are—in total love. Giving total and complete love is Jesus' job. No one can do that for us but Him. The purpose of getting real and honest with another person is so that we can experience redemption and restoration at a social level, with other human beings.

It's been suggested that we choose someone of the same gender. This is not a hard and fast rule but, especially where sexual issues or addictions are involved, we will probably feel more at ease with someone of the same gender. Pastors and members of the clergy usually work quite well, but not always. Competent counselors, therapists or the appropriate mental health professionals should be considered. They can usually be very helpful in matters related to recovery from addiction. We want to find someone we trust, someone who is able keep all that we have to tell them in complete confidence. Above all, we want to find someone who exemplifies the love and acceptance of Jesus. The person we choose to speak with needs to be confident in our ability to recover based on the power of God's love. They need to believe that Jesus' love can help all people, especially those of us who are working to recover from our addictions. In many ways, our listener becomes our advocate at a personal and social level, much like Jesus is our advocate with God. A person who has suffered from and is recovering from an addiction is often a very good choice. Most of all, we need to find someone who is capable of looking past whatever self-deception that still holds us back. And, at the same time, our listener needs to see us for who we really are, like God sees us. It is important that they not ignore the remaining personal dishonesty that we still have. We need them to be understanding and patient with us at the same time, too.

Once we have found someone who we feel comfortable with, we need to tell that person the reason why we feel the need to have a serious discussion with them. Respectfully, we'll ask him or her for their time. We need to tell that person that we are working to recover from an addiction and that we need help from others to do so. We should explain that it may take more than one appointment. These conversations cannot be rushed if they are to be effective. It is important that we express our desire to have a growing faith in God and trusting relationships with other people. It is also important that we explain that we are committing ourselves to be as honest in our conversations as we can be.

We need to tell our listener about what we have habitually thought about ourselves, other people and God. Speaking to another person about our deepest reality means that we do not discuss the faults and mistakes of other people. Right now, at this point in time, problems and faults of others are not our concern. Focusing on the problems that other people have created for us will only deepen our resentment and anger. Let's stick with the facts about ourselves.

Often, our greatest motivation will be the pain that our addictions have brought into our lives. Reaching out for all the goodness that God has, let us make the most of this opportunity, and this day, so that we can recover from our addictions and—best of all—experience all of the goodness that God gives.

Light Shines Before Us

"You can't whitewash your sins and get by with it; you find mercy by admitting and leaving them. A tenderhearted person lives a blessed life; a hardhearted person lives a hard life."
            Proverbs 28:13 -14 *The Message*

"Honest men fear neither the light nor the dark."
      - Thomas Fuller, M.D.

Admitted to God, to ourselves and to another human being the exact nature of our wrongs.

Once we have been honest and real with another person, we should take some time for personal reflection. Taking the time to reflect gives us the chance to look back over the spectrum of our recovery experience and absorb more deeply all that has been happening in our minds and in our hearts. We'll want to thank God and our listener for the love and the acceptance they have given to us. We should also acknowledge ourselves for being courageous and determined in our recovery work. Reflecting back, we can begin to see that God has been beside us all along. He was with us in the conversation that we had with our listener, and even before that. Now, we can begin to see that He's been reaching out to us, even before our recovery began. For you see, God is always one step ahead of us. He is always there, waiting for us to show up, honestly sharing with Him the truths of who we really are.

The conversation that we had with our listener has been a real "first" for most of us. Now, having had this "first of its kind" experience, we can sit quietly, alone and at peace, experiencing our bodies, our minds and our hearts being comfortable and at rest with one another. The angst, the resentment and the ongoing distrust that we have felt for ourselves and others can now begin to slip into the past. We can sense a new kind of feeling. We can feel that the world we live in is a good world and that we are a valuable part of the goodness that God makes. Thank God for our Step Five experience. Let's continually ask Him to help us grow in honesty. Let's ask Him to help us to let go of the remaining burdens that we place on ourselves and others.

Journaling what we have discovered is important so that we don't forget the past. We are more likely to end up where we don't want to be if we forget where we've already been. Also, sharing our experience with those in our recovery fellowship helps us to keep moving forward, too. With this kind of progress, we will sense a new kind of confidence deep inside of us. We won't be alone anymore. We have seen a glimpse of God's accepting love, and we have experienced the joy of having someone else know our secrets and not turn away. Knowing that we are accepted by God and another person helps us to change. We can accept ourselves, failures and all. Redemption has begun. To the degree that we recognize and accept the value that God has for us, we will recognize, accept and value ourselves, too.

We can see that our future will be different from the past. While still capable of addictive self-destruction, we know that the downward spirals that we have known before are no longer inevitable. We can live large, in a world of imperfect but wonderful people who—when honest with God and others—make themselves available to be loved by a strength and a power that is capable of giving life amid all hardship and sorrow. Sharing is caring. We become living miracles in the lives of others when we share honestly.

Step Six

We became entirely ready to have God remove all these defects of character.

Step Six is not about doing, it is about being—being *ready*. While not the active hands-on kind of work of Steps Four and Five, Step Six is never passive; it requires an active commitment of the will. It is an intentional giving up of what we think we are entitled to, and giving up what we expect in the future. At the same time, in Step Six God makes us ready to be changed into a fundamentally different kind of person than who we have been in the past.

Ultimately, it is God who changes us. But, we are, at the same time, responsible for living in such a way that the changes that God wants to make in us are possible. Living differently—in faith, that is—the process of change happens inside of us beginning with the way that we think about ourselves, about God and about other people. Thinking differently helps us to react and respond differently in the future. Change happens over time, the results of which are more dramatic and more apparent at some times and in some ways than others. The schedule for interpersonal change is dictated by God. All we can do is to live out our lives in obedient cooperation with Him. We must be willing to let go of our expectations, especially our expectations of "religious excellence." Our goal, after all, is to absorb more of the life of Christ, not just to behave like Christ, if that were even possible.

Christ will make us into *the real deal* if we let Him.

Dissatisfaction and Desire

"Blessed are those who hunger and thirst for righteousness… "
Matthew 5:6 *NLT*

"Discontent is holy when it compels us to dream of redemption."
- Dan Allender, Ph.D.

We became entirely ready to have God remove all these defects of character.

Being part of a recovery fellowship on an ongoing basis will provide us with many opportunities to hear others tell about how they have suffered because of their addictions, and what it has been like for them to find recovery. One of the most incredible and amazing things that we will ever experience in a meeting is when someone shares how he or she has become grateful for having had addictions. In recovery, it is possible for the pain of our addictions to become a great motivator in our lives. Pain keeps us moving forward, compelling us to keep reaching out to find answers for the pain and troubles of life. As we recover, we find a very simple but profound solution. The solution for us is to want God—to want what He has to give us, more than we want what we, or our addictions, can provide us. This new kind of God-given desire helps us to see that pain is not our enemy, and we don't need to run from it anymore. As we become wiling to face the day-to-day pains of life, our pain and difficulties are transformed into powerful avenues of learning and growth. Embracing pain as a learning opportunity brings us face-to-face with God's work of redemption—a work that is only available to those who have the deep, pliable humility that leeches out of a desperate and dying pain.

We all seem to want more out of life than what we can provide for ourselves. Not only do we fail to supply ourselves with the *things* that we think will make us happy; our addictions prove that we fail to provide ourselves with a satisfying level of interpersonal and spiritual connectedness, too. We all fall short. We all fail to meet our own needs. By recognizing how we have failed to meet our own needs, no matter how hard we tried, we can see that the *things* that we've been addicted to are not our biggest problem. Our real problem is who we *are*. We are all in need of a complete, interpersonal overhaul, starting with the very core of our minds, our hearts and our innermost character.

Our addictions grow from a deep personal longing inside of us that silently cries out to be touched. When our deep longing goes untouched, we cry out all the more in ever deeper ways, craving with increasing intensity for more of the *things* that brought us relief in the past. This is how our addictions take hold of us. Deep-rooted painful feelings of uselessness, worthlessness and loneliness can be the triggers that send us back to our addictions time after time. With our longing unsatisfied, and after numerous and repeated attempts to do the right thing, invariably we fail, once again, falling deeper into our addictions. Desperate, over time, we become wholly and completely dissatisfied with who we are and with the way we have lived our lives. Our good intentions and our failures have simmered together until, finally—with God's help—we become entirely ready to be recreated into a fundamentally different kind of person. We are sick and tired of being sick and tired. We are convinced that we will never satisfy our own innermost needs. Staying the same is no longer acceptable to us. We want to be different. Deep in our hearts we know that if we do not humbly make the choice to change, we will eventually die still wallowing in our addictions.

This profound misery and discontent is the birth point of a new healthier desire—a desire based not on our previous loves or lusts, but on a healthy and compelling longing to experience new life inside of us. The pain of our addictions helps us to understand that we really don't need *things* to change; rather, the "I", the "ME", and the "WE" need to change. We are no longer satisfied with just being healed from our addictions. We want to have our complete and total self reformatted and changed by the perfect design of God.

Ready and Listening

"The people I love, I call to account--prod and correct and guide so that they'll live at their best. Up on your feet, then! About face! Run after God! Look at me. I stand at the door. I knock. If you hear me call and open the door, I'll come right in and sit down to supper with you."
    Revelation 3:19-20 *The Message*

"The teacher is heard when the student is ready to listen."
    - Ancient Chinese Proverb

We became entirely ready to have God remove all these defects of character.

We so often miss out on the deep moving of God's Spirit because we are not available. Most of us live in a fog spiritually. God knocks and either we are not at home or we are too lazy or distracted to get up out of our easy chair to see who is at the door. God speaks to us—and all of mankind—through Scripture. The message of Scripture is meant to be assimilated as a love letter, one person at a time, yet we so often think of it as just history, teaching or principle. Scripture is certainly all that, but it is so much more. God's Scripture is a calling of love and redemption. It is the ancient record of God communicating to us, individually and collectively, as people. Scripture is a love letter. It is a timeless record of how God wants to connect with us and draw us close. God has been speaking to us so very often and for so long, yet most of the time we have not responded.

Being ready to change means that we will want to be, first and foremost, in a love-fulfilling relationship with God. To some degree we are completely aware of how far away we are from this ideal. We tend to get so caught up in telling God where we want to go with our lives that we make ourselves blind and oblivious to the idolatrous ways that we try to sculpt and mold our own souls. If we stand around waiting for God to dump some sort of monumental task and duty on us, we will miss the powerfully subtle opportunities for change and transformation that God has already set before us. Those whose ears are not tuned to hear the quiet voice of God do not change. If we want to hear, we have to be willing to listen. The man or woman who strains to hear the quiet and sometimes seemingly distant call of love and change is the one who gains the great prize of a transformed life experience. Rarely does it occur to us that what God really wants us to do is to live out His transforming power in all the most mundane ways. It is critically important that we give up every form of grandiosity and recognize that God's greatest work has to do with how we live our daily lives. He is more concerned with transforming us in the ways we interact with our families, run our errands, conduct our careers and live in our neighborhoods than He is in some sort of dramatic conquest. In real life, the greatest conquests are experienced in 24-hour segments right in the center of our routine everyday life.

The bottom line of true character transformation is understanding that God redeems people, not things. Then, as people experience God's transforming redemption, His redemption is reflected in all areas of that person's life. Becoming ready for God to change us means that we don't have to *get* ready. We just have to be willing to be ready. We stay alert, listening for our Master Redeemer's call. Changing us is God's job. Our job is to simply be ready and willing to change.

The scriptural record of Moses' life is a picture of a person who was made ready to change, even though he was seemingly unaware of the preparation that God had made in his life. The burning bush was God's way of reaching out and capturing the willingness that Moses had in his heart—a willingness that he was previously incapable of acting on in healthy and productive ways. Scripture tells of how Moses had apparently lost all confidence in himself, and of how God used the humbling circumstances and consequences of Moses' life to make him ready and willing to hear what God had to say. Moses' willing, albeit hesitant response to God's call is definitive proof that he was ready for whatever God had for him.

Becoming Ready

"When the Lord saw that he had caught Moses' attention, God called to him from the bush, 'Moses! Moses!'
'Here I am!' Moses replied."
      Exodus 3:4

"Since most of us are born with an abundance of natural desires, it isn't strange that we often let these far exceed their intended purpose. When they drive us blindly, or we willfully demand that they supply us with more satisfactions or pleasures than are possible or due us, that is the point at which we depart from the degree of perfection that God wishes for us here on earth. That is the measure of our character defects or if you wish, of our sins."
      - Alcoholics Anonymous

We became entirely ready to have God remove all these defects of character.

The way that God deals with us on a personal level will be as unique as we are as individuals and as mysterious as God is himself. While we all share common ground with one another, we will have some very specific and unique experiences that will prepare us for the life that God has planned for us. What God uses to get hold of one person may not work for another. No matter how it happens, each of us will be led—if we are not already there—into a wilderness experience. Our hopes will be lost and our dreams will be destroyed. We will be reduced to the helpless and dependent state of a child. As painful and difficult as this may sound, this is all good news, because only in a childlike experience of dependency can we be made ready to receive the best that God has to give us.

Our friend Moses is one example of how God pulled someone into a life-changing encounter with himself. As a young man, Moses had a difficult time staying out of trouble. Conflict seemed to follow him wherever he went. He seemed to be at his best and at his worst when he was responding to the people and the circumstances around him. Moses had a strong desire to change the things that he thought were wrong, but very often his best intentions—combined with his misguided reactions—made things worse. Moses used his God-given talents in ways that were both bad and good. Moses was, in himself, conflicted, just like we are.

The story of Moses' life is told in the biblical books of Exodus and Deuteronomy. These books paint a colorful picture of a man who had all the best intentions, and at the same time they also show us a man who had a painfully difficult time turning his good intentions into healthy and productive action. Moses' character defects often blocked the good outcomes that he intended. We need to read the biblical record in order to see the complete picture of Moses' life, but here are a few low and high points of interest that will help us to see how God worked to change Moses' thinking—which in turn changed Moses' way of living.

Born an Israelite and separated from his parents as an infant, Moses was raised by the daughter of the king of Egypt. He was educated by the best that the culture of his day had to offer. One day as a young man, seeing one of his Hebrew countrymen being beaten, Moses went to his countryman's aid and killed an Egyptian citizen. Later, when Moses was confronted about the killing, he fled into the wilderness in order to escape prosecution for the murder that he committed. There, in the wilderness, he married and started a family, and he lived in obscurity. In his running away, Moses abandoned himself to the wilderness. He abandoned his lost hopes and his broken dreams. But God did not abandon Moses. After many years, the king of Egypt died. Moses, who was now tending sheep for his father-in-law, had given up and maybe forgotten all about his ideas of heroic acts. But God had not forgotten, and God had certainly not given up on Moses. God was at work deep in Moses' heart and mind during this time of obscurity. God was preparing him for the future that He had in mind for him. When God's work of preparation was fulfilled, He reached out and made contact with Moses through the burning bush. When God spoke, Moses, having been made ready in ways that he was not even aware of, answered back to God. Then, because he was ready and willing, Moses set out to become all that God had prepared him to be. As a result of God's work of preparation—coupled with Moses' humble willingness to change—Moses returned to Egypt, where he led his Israelite brothers and sisters out of a captivity they had suffered for over 400 years. (Please read Exodus Chapter 3 for a more detailed account of how all this happened.)

Like Moses, we have spent years living in obscurity and pain, as proven by our addictions. We never meant to end up the way we were, but we did. We never intended to get sidetracked, but we did. Our addictions prove how we had given up on ourselves, how we had lost our hopes and our dreams. But—and here is the good news—God has not given up on us. He is at work. He is sustaining our lives and He is waiting for us to be ready to have the defects in our character removed from us.

Our good intentions and our character defects are like two sides of the same coin. They live together, side by side, until we become entirely ready to have the character defects that corrupt our good intentions removed from us. This means that we are ready to be made into fundamentally different people. Staying the same will no longer be acceptable to us. We want to be different in order to move on and experience the life that God has to give us.

Feeling dissatisfied with who we are creates a deep desire for change. Dissatisfaction and desire go hand-in-hand, much like our good intentions and our character defects. The kind of dissatisfaction that leads to desire for change makes us intentional about our recovery. It motivates us to take action. The desire that we feel for change is a gift from God. It is a quality that is unique to the human experience. It reveals the redeemable condition of our heart. Godly dissatisfaction and the desire to change create a vision for how we will live—not only recovering from our addictions, but as men and women who are truly free. Godly desire is about becoming ready to have the entire panorama of our inner life reformatted and changed by the perfect design of God. Godly desire makes us ready to set aside our own demands for personal satisfaction. It makes us ready to be the kind of people who love other people in ways that only God makes possible. Our old nature will dry up and begin to fall away. We will bloom from the inside out. We will realize that we are prepared—or maybe it is better to say that we are *being* prepared—to live life in a way that only God can empower us to do. Just like our friend, Moses.

The story of Moses' life is a wonderful example of how God makes good use of our failures. It is safe to say that Moses was better prepared by God during the time that he spent living in obscurity than in any way that Moses could have ever prepared himself. Just like with Moses, God is doing His most intimate work inside of us during the times when we feel the most broken and hopeless. It is during times of difficulty and failure that God whittles away at our ego and prepares our character to become more like His own. We can't always see or feel this most intimate work of God, but its reality is proven through our own willingness—the willingness to change that we now have but did not have before.

Nothing is ever wasted if we are willing to give it to God. The more God rules our minds and our hearts, the more our failures and addictions will become assets to us and to those around us.

What We Really Need

"If you will throw away your detestable idols and go astray no more, and if you swear by my name alone, and begin to live good lives and uphold justice, then you will be a blessing to the nations of the world, and all people will come and praise my name."
Jeremiah 4:1, *The Message*

"To admit discontent and hunger for redemption requires that we face our part in the problem and compels us to yearn and dream of more."
- Dan Allender, Ph.D.

We became entirely ready to have God remove all these defects of character.

Very often we get confused about what we really need because we are obsessed with what we want. As addicted and self-centered people, we tend to have distorted perceptions of our own personal needs. One of our great challenges is to understand that our God-given instincts for intimate love, relational security and eternal acceptance are all that we really need, and that only God can meet these needs. Part of the psychological insanity of any addiction is that—at least at some level—we believe that we need or depend on things that are unreliable and destructive. In almost every case, we've been at fault for either denying our needs, or for demanding that our needs be met in ways that are inappropriate, given God's design for our lives.

Our destructive reliances blind us in such a way that it is very difficult for us to see how our self-centeredness is the cause of all our character defects and all of our sins. Worrying and feeling sorry for ourselves will destroy us. Self-pity and self-idolatry are deadly. *Self-centered* thinking gets us into trouble because self-centered thoughts are prompted by fear, even when we are not aware that we are feeling fearful. Because of this, it is very important that we learn not to impulsively act on our first thought. It is important that we learn to think through things in order to think clearly and act appropriately. Part of recovery is learning to think *faith*-fully, not *fear*-fully. Just because our head sits on our shoulders does not mean it is our friend.

Feelings of personal inferiority or superiority, grandiose beliefs of entitlement, self-centered motives and priorities are all symptoms of the deeper problem of self-centeredness. When we believe that our demands *must* be met, or that it's bad or wrong to feel discomfort or have difficulty, or that others are here to make us happy, we reveal ourselves as the selfish center of our own lives. In recovery and faith, God allows us an ever-increasing abundance of choices for goodness and personal prosperity. There is only one true wrong, and that is to make ourselves the center of our own world. God has never shared His position of authority with anyone, and He won't share it with us. All of our character defects and all of our sins come from our silly attempts to rule our own "kingdom." On the other hand, as we learn to focus our mind, our heart, our desires and our intentions on God, we will find the willingness to let go of our character defects, to let go of our addictions and even to let go of the habitual sinfulness that has held us back in life. Even the smallest example of faith, no matter how small or seemingly inconsequential, pleases God. Once the seed of readiness and change is planted inside of us—and no one can do this for us; we must do it for ourselves—our recovery partners and fellowship will help us to identify, nurture and grow these seedlings of positive change.

"Faith as small as a mustard seed" Matthew 17:20

At the end of all things and considerations, only God will prove to be completely reliable. Only God will prove to be completely healthy and life-giving. Any reliance that is not centered on God is potentially idolatrous, destructive and addictive. On the other hand, a healthy reliance on God can never be idolatrous, it can never be destructive, and it can never be addictive.

Emotional Triggers

"You're blessed when you get your inside world--your mind and heart--put right. Then you can see God in the outside world."
Matthew 5:8 *The Message*

"No matter what we do or where we hide, we can't escape our essential design. We long to be free of shame's restraints, immersed in the passion of giving and receiving. We long to live a sacrificial life that matters today and tomorrow."
- Dan Allender, Ph.D.

We became entirely ready to have God remove all these defects of character.

It is a good idea for us to review our Step Four inventory along with our sponsor or counselor. When doing this review with an open mind and heart, we can begin to see how difficult emotions can be triggers for our addictions. While emotions can be our triggers, our character defects are the building blocks of addiction, and our self-centeredness is the cement which holds our addictive nature together. We will never find the freedom to recover and live well until these addictive components are removed from us.

In reviewing our inventory, we can see how our character defects began innocently when we were children. They were our means of survival. We learned to manipulate to get our needs met. We lied to protect ourselves. We hid our emotions to avoid embarrassment and shame. We rationalized things in order to escape ugly realities that were too much for us to bear alone. Our character defects are really ineffective tools for coping and control. They are our methods of minimizing pain and diffusing threats that we see coming our way. Without realizing it, our character defects have become a kind of strategy to care for ourselves when we are afraid no one else will.

We may feel afraid when we think of losing our defective coping mechanisms. After all, we have—at least to some degree—subconsciously thought that our character defects were important for us to survive. Thinking this way, we will subconsciously mourn the thought of having our character defects removed from us. Because letting go of our character defects can be painful, it is important that we lean on those who have been working at recovery longer than we have. Those who have more experience will understand our pain and fear. Fearing the loss of a coping mechanism is understandable, but it is essential for us to grieve these losses without complaint so that we can effectively move on down the path of recovery.

Exercising courage makes it possible to learn new and healthy ways to live our lives without resorting to the addictions that we have relied on in the past. With courage, we trade our destructive emotions and addictions for the simple gift of gratitude. Gratitude posts a guard at the door of our hearts, which is to be accessed only by God and those whom He allows. Gratitude will help us to be thankful for life as it is, not how we wish it or expect it to be.

Today and every day, we stand at a crossroads. But we don't stand alone. Our recovery fellowship stands with us. Even better, the Source of all power— God—has joined the battle for us to live a new way, to become new people, to be free.

Becoming Aware

"Good friend, don't forget all I've taught you, take to heart my commands. They'll help you live a long, long time, a long life lived full and well."

Proverbs 3:1-2 *The Message*

"A fault which humbles a man is of more use to him than a good action which puffs him up."

- Thomas Wilson

We became entirely ready to have God remove all these defects of character.

One of the payoffs of our recovery effort is seeing how our previous Twelve Step work pays dividends. Our recovery work becomes our second best friend (our best friend is God and His grace), when we persist with it. Referring back to the personal inventory that we did in Step Four and the journaling that we did after we admitted our wrongs in Step Five will give us a good bit of insight as to how the defects in our character manifest themselves. Our previous work gives us a platform from which we can see our emotional and mental landscape from a broader point of view. Our character defects will appear in bold print when we are ready to see them and do something about them. Recognizing our shortcomings shows that we are seeing ourselves in a more honest and sincere way. Identifying our flawed thinking, misguided believing and self–centered acting is vital for the future of our recovery and our lives. This is an incredibly important part of our recovery effort.

Here are some questions that can help us get a better view of how our character defects can be hidden away in plain sight in our everyday lives.

Do I have difficulty asking for help?   *Pride*
Am I in debt or do I prefer my desires over other's?   *Greed*

Am I upset when someone is more privileged than me?	*Jealousy*
Am I afraid?	*Fear*
Who am I mad at?	*Resentment*
What am I mad about?	*Entitlement*
Do I feel the need to please someone other than God?	*Approval seeking*
Do I get frustrated when others don't act as I want?	*Controlling others*
Do I fear being alone?	*Dependency on others*
Am I uncomfortable around others?	*Isolation*
Do I feel nervous for no particular reason?	*Insecurity*
Do I prefer to work when I should be elsewhere?	*Being a workaholic*
Do I feel the need to keep secrets?	*Dishonesty*
Am I eating in an unhealthy manner?	*Gluttony*
Am I upset when others have what I do not?	*Envy*
Do I procrastinate?	*Laziness*
Do I think my life will change without me changing?	*Fanciful Thinking*

It is quite easy to *feel* recovered, to get complacent and to forget the insidious nature of our addictions. We must never forget that there's still some very important work that needs to be done. There are more questions to be asked. Monitoring ourselves and recognizing our character defects provides us with a very caring and loving insight into our own lives. How have our character defects impacted the lives of others? Did our selfish and prideful actions turn out well for us or for anyone else? Do we now display kindness and goodness? Why not?

Honestly recognizing our real world behaviors and attitudes will provide us with improved personal judgment for our present and future actions. Forgetting these important lessons learned is catastrophic for anyone who is attempting to recover from an addiction.

Reversing the Past

"I'm single-minded in pursuit of you; don't let me miss the road signs you've posted. I've banked your promises in the vault of my heart so I won't sin myself bankrupt. Be blessed, GOD; train me in your ways of wise living."

> Psalm 119:10-12 *The Message*

"When our desire is focused on loving God and others, we will realize our deepest longings for life fulfilled."

> - An Anonymous Recovering Alcoholic

We became entirely ready to have God remove all these defects of character.

None of us will ever eliminate our character defects on our own, no matter how hard we try. While it is not possible for us to remove our character defects on our own, we can learn to change the way we think, the way we act and the way we live our lives. Letting go of character defects is never passive. Like everything else we do in recovery, character change requires action. Personal growth and change is a divine interaction between God's grace and our choices. When we change our actions, we interrupt habitual patterns of thinking, believing and feeling. Motion changes emotion!

It takes some practice, but with a little commitment and a few failures (which we will want to share with another person), the changes to the way we think, feel and act will begin to come quite quickly. People from religious backgrounds call this *repentance* and that's exactly what it is— grassroots, down and dirty, rubber meets the road repentance. The simplest definition of repentance is to "change one's mind." It's an *about-face*—turning and going in the other direction. Whatever you call it, it works.

Scripture offers an overwhelming abundance of practical insight and guidance for those of us who are looking for renewal and strength. Some things simply cannot be said any better than Scripture has already said it.

"And so I insist – and God backs me up on this – that there be no going along with the crowd, the *empty-headed*, mindless crowd. They've refused for so long to deal with God that they've lost touch not only with God but with reality itself. They can't think straight anymore. Feeling no pain, they let themselves go in sexual obsession, addicted to every sort of perversion. But that's no life for you! You learned Christ! My assumption is that you have paid careful attention to him, been well instructed in the truth precisely as we have it in Jesus. Since then, we do not have the excuse of ignorance, everything – and I do mean everything – connected with that old way of life has to go. It's rotten through and through. Get rid of it! And then take on an entirely new way of life – a *God-fashioned* life, a life renewed from the inside working itself into your conduct as God accurately reproduces his character in you."
Ephesians 4:19 - 23 *The Message*

Any questions?

Step Seven

We humbly asked Him to remove our shortcomings.

Our recovery program must be built on the development and growth of personal humility if we are to be successful. Because of this, it is important that we understand what humility is. Humility is a realistic understanding of who we are and how we relate with God, other people and the world around us. It is a deep commitment to interpersonal truth. Humility necessitates that we maintain an ongoing examination of our thoughts, our feelings and our actions in order for us to keep a healthy and balanced self-awareness. This builds integrity in the way we think and act. Humility is what causes us to see ourselves as sinners that God is working to redeem. Humility helps us to have a healthier understanding of how we fit into the world so that we can freely interact with God and other people on all levels. Humility allows us to understand the power of God in more personal and practical ways.

Step Seven is an ongoing request that is born of humility. It comes from a growing confidence in God, a balanced appreciation for others, and a sincere conviction that we will never solve the deep problems in our character by ourselves. We have to have help. In Step Seven, we humbly ask God to do for us what we can never do for ourselves.

Let us always remember that the first word in Step Seven is "we."

From Shame to Grace

"For God can use sorrow in our lives to help us turn away from sin and seek salvation. We will never regret that kind of sorrow. But sorrow without repentance is the kind that results in death."
2 Corinthians 7:10, NLT

"We can accept God's good gifts too easily. Grace can be accepted only when we face our own inabilities. Forgiveness can be embraced only when we lay bare our wrongdoing, and hope can be imparted only when we face the reality of our own despair."
- Charles Ringma

We humbly asked Him to remove our shortcomings.

Humility is an awareness that we are both imperfect and worthwhile at the same time. Humility is a high ground that traverses the bogs and swamps of grandiosity and self-hatred. Humility chooses to follow God's plan over our own. When we live humbly—which can be defined as *consistently choosing God's way of doing things over our own way of doing things*—impossibly good things begin to happen to otherwise impossible people like us. We get turned inside out. Our attitude begins to change. Our outlook on life becomes healthier and more balanced. The destructive feelings we have had for ourselves will diminish. We will begin to see things differently. As we change on the inside, things around us begin to change as well. Life and the way we live it begin to make sense.

Humility is an acceptance of ourselves, sin and all. Humility helps us to see ourselves with one eye to evaluate and the other eye to appreciate. Humility admits shortcomings and wrongdoing, and then reaches out and accepts the help that is needed to make serious changes. Humility helps us to understand the problems that we cannot solve on our own. This is why Jesus becomes increasingly important to us in our recovery. For you see, God never expects us to solve all of our problems on our own. He understands that our character defects and our addictions are beyond our ability to change. So, God offers to do for us what we can never do for ourselves. He offers to transform us by taking our character defects and, in exchange, replacing them with the character of Jesus. All we have to do is give up our character defects to Him and humbly receive Jesus' character as God, according to His plan, builds it in us.

Facing the Facts

"Humble yourselves under the mighty hand of God, that He may exalt you in due time, casting all your care upon Him, for He cares for you."
I Peter 5:6-7

"For just so long as we were convinced that we could live exclusively by our own individual strength and intelligence, for just that long was a working faith in a Higher Power impossible. This was true even when we believed God existed. We could actually have earnest religious beliefs which remained barren because we were still trying to play God ourselves. As long as we placed self-reliance first, a genuine reliance upon a Higher Power was out of the question. That basic ingredient of all humility, a desire to seek and do God's will was missing."
- Big Book of Alcoholics Anonymous

We humbly asked Him to remove our shortcomings.

For most of us, our first encounter with real humility was when we admitted that we had an addiction that was more powerful than we were. We have grown in humility as we have worked through our Step Four personal inventory. This kind of recovery work makes it possible for us to humbly *'own'* the truth about ourselves. When we see and accept the real facts about our choices and our lives, we will be less inclined to rationalize our improper actions, minimize our difficulties or ignore the pain that other people have suffered because of our character defects. Knowing the real facts about ourselves helps us to see our own limitations and to accept the blunt truth of our needs and shortcomings. We are not all-powerful. We don't control ourselves all of the time, and we do not control other people any of the time. Humility helps us to accept these facts, giving us eyes through which we'll see God change who we are, the way we think, the way we handle our emotions and the way we live our lives.

The growth and maturity we experience is one of the gifts of humility that God will give to us as we responsibly admit and correct our character defects. It looks like this. When we notice a character defect expressed through our thoughts and actions, we make the choice to reverse our thinking and our actions. When we do so, our character defects will begin to lose some of their power. Every time we say 'no' to them, the grip they've habitually had on us loosens. Nothing is so helpful to curing addictions and healing character defects as to stop doing the addiction and admit the character defects that have been a part of our addictive thinking. An amazing empowerment from God comes with obedience.

As we progress in our recovery, our priorities and concerns will get reorganized. With a measure much greater than our obedience, we will be given the humility to desire obedience more than blessing, character more than comfort—all so that we may help and not hinder the work of God. The greatest blessing for any of us is to live free from our addiction and be fully aligned with the will of a loving God. Even before we ask, God is giving us all that we have ever needed. He is always one step ahead of us!

Humbly Asking

"God's kingdom is like a treasure hidden in a field for years and then accidentally found by a trespasser. The finder is ecstatic – what a find! – and proceeds to sell everything he owns to raise money and buy that field."

>   Matthew 13:44 *The Message*

"So in terms of what every man needs most crucially, all man's power is powerless because at its roots, of course, the deepest longing of the human soul is the longing for God, and this no man has the power to satisfy."

>   - Frederick Buechner

We humbly asked Him to remove our shortcomings.

How many times have we asked God to give us patience only to get mad with ourselves or God when patience didn't show up when we wanted it? Perhaps we really weren't interested in being more patient. Maybe what we really wanted was relief from the tension and discomfort that we were feeling at that time. In light of what we are learning now, we will probably find it much more helpful to simply admit to ourselves, to God and to another person that we are impatient by nature and that we want to change. We want to learn to think and to act differently—*patiently.* This is real world humility. This kind of openness helps us to have a more natural willingness to ask others for direction and then to responsibly follow whatever good advice we get.

Saying, "Dear God, I want to be more patient," sounds good, but we may miss the subtle demand that we are making—holding God responsible for our impatient character and problems. But when we say "Dear God, I am an impatient person," we offer the truth about ourselves and we accept responsibility for being impatient. *Humbly asking* means asking for changes to our character and thinking with no demand for changes in the external circumstances of our lives.

The ultimate purpose of all prayer is to get hold of God. To do so we have to let go of our pride, inviting God to act according to His purpose in our lives. Changes in our circumstances are optional; changes in our character are necessary. We become the changes we desire. God will be our strength and He will empower us to do what we are responsible to do.

Humility Through and Through

"Don't copy the behavior and customs of this world, but let God transform you into a new person by changing the way you think. Then you will know what God wants you to do, and you will know how good and pleasing and perfect his will is."
  Romans 12:2, *NLT*

"My Creator, I am now willing that you should have all of me, good and bad. I pray that you now remove from me every single defect of character which stands in the way of my usefulness to you and my fellows. Grant me strength, as I go out from here, to do your bidding. Amen."
  - Step Seven Prayer from The Big Book of A A

We humbly asked Him to remove our shortcomings.

There is a terrible fear that we will all feel at some time in our life. This is the fear that we are alone and that no one will care for us in a way that will make us feel secure and meaningful. This fear, this aloneness, can feel spiritually fatal. This kind of fear cultivates and facilitates our addictions. It reduces us to shame-filled and fearful little boys and girls.

As we admit these intimate and painful feelings of ours, we begin to realize that God has been wanting us and waiting for us all along no matter how we felt or what we feared. We discover—through His grace coupled with our faith—that He has been working to make a transforming connection with us. Realizing this, we are better able to lay hold of a life and a goodness that was impossible before we admitted our need for His help. Pursuing this strength and freedom that He gives, we willingly let go of the character defects that have kept us from "knowing the measure and stature of Christ" (please see Ephesians 4:13).

Where we had once been ruled by our lusts, by our addictions and by other people, today we are becoming men and women who admit our character defects and—at the same time—we are uncovering the treasure of God's imminent presence in our lives. It is through humility and faith that we receive the transforming spirit of Christ. Christ empowers us with a love that is our only ruler today. It is the rule of God's love.

Our relationship with God must always be more important to us than career, hobbies, church, even family and friends. Character building and spiritual values must come first if we want to continue to recover from our addictions. Without recovery nothing else will matter, because nothing else will survive our addictions. All that is good stays good only with God's love and care coupled with our humble heart. Without Him, there is nothing worth having.

The Source of Our Strength

"And we are confident that he hears us whenever we ask for anything that pleases him. And since we know he hears us when we make our requests, we also know that he will give us what we ask for."
 I John 5:14,15 *NLT*

"A great turning point in our lives came when we sought for humility as something we really wanted, rather than as something we must have. It marked the time when we could commence to see the full implication of Step Seven."
 - Big Book of Alcoholics Anonymous

We humbly asked Him to remove our shortcomings.

We have, albeit unintentionally, created the problems that we have in our character. Now we are asking God, with as much humility as possible, to resolve the problems that stand in the way of us experiencing all that God has for us. Before, we had spent much of our lives and energy attempting to overcome what we could never overcome in our own power. But today, as we surrender our lives to God and humbly ask Him to remove our shortcomings, we discover a strength that is unlike anything that we have ever encountered before. Only in God, and through the help of others, will we receive the strength and the endurance to continuously let go of our character defects and our addictions.

Nothing in our recovery work is magical or unreal. We will forever be human and prone to all of our human inadequacies. As much as we may wish it to be different, not all of our character defects will be removed from us. The work that God is doing in our hearts and minds will be part of His overall purposes. We will help ourselves the most when we accept the consequences that we have created for ourselves without complaint, so that we can enjoy the benefit of lessons learned once and for all.

There will be times when we try to get rid of our character defects and fail, sometimes repeatedly. We will inevitably find ourselves in situations where we have to choose between trusting God amidst our repeated attempts of trying and failing, and the certain penalty of failing to try, which is in and of itself a failure to trust God. What we choose to do with failure is perhaps the most profound indicator of who we are and who we will become. Failure with effort can be a frustrating setback. The setbacks and disappointments create the sad feeling inside of us that we may never overcome our problems. This is where we will need help from our friends in recovery and from God himself. We will have our setbacks. We will try and fail sometimes. But, let us stay honest and let us stay motivated because our own fatal failure is giving up. Failure to try is suicide. It is here—in our failures and setbacks—that we learn to keep turning to God, time after time, and in so doing we learn to experience Him to be our Source, our Strength and our Joy.

Changing the Way We Live

"It is obvious what kind of life develops out of trying to get your own way all the time: repetitive, loveless, cheap sex; a stinking accumulation of mental and emotional garbage; frenzied and joyless grabs for happiness; trinket gods; magic-show religion; paranoid loneliness; cutthroat competition; all consuming-yet-never-satisfied wants; a brutal temper; an impotence to love or be loved; divided homes and lives; small-minded and lopsided pursuits; the vicious habit of depersonalizing everyone into a rival; uncontrolled and uncontrollable addictions, ugly parodies of community. I could go on. This isn't the first time I have warned you, you know. If you use your freedom this way, you will not inherit God's kingdom. But what happens when we live God's way? He brings gifts into our lives, much the same way that fruit appears in an orchard – things like affection for others, exuberance for life, serenity. We develop a willingness to stick with things, a sense of compassion in the heart, and a conviction that a basic holiness permeates things and people. We find ourselves involved in loyal commitments, not needing to force our way in life, able to marshal and direct our energies wisely."
Galatians 5:19–23 *The Message*

"A fault which humbles a man is of more use to him than a good action which puffs him up."
- Thomas Wilson

We humbly asked Him to remove our shortcomings.

It is dangerous to be unwilling to relinquish one of our character defects; it potentially sabotages our entire recovery effort. At the very least it limits our future. When we feel like we are hanging onto a character defect that we don't want to let go of, let us admit our doubt, our fear, and the struggle and stubbornness that we know is inside of us. We admit these things to ourselves, to God and to another person. Let us pray while we admit these things, asking for God's help in relieving us of the fear and pride that weigh us down. Let us ask God to help us let go of everything that stands between us and a closer relationship with Him.

Praying in this way assures us that we will receive what we ask for, because we are praying for what we know to be God's will for us. Knowing that God will be working in us in this way does not take away our responsibility for taking appropriate actions to deal with our character defects. We must always be people of action—*effective* action. When we have doubts about our conduct or character, we will find it helpful to speak with our sponsor or someone else who knows about our addictions and our desire to recover. Letting go of our character defects begins with prayer, but it also includes acting and living as if God has already equipped us (and He has) to live well without them. Prayer without action is little more than mental, emotional and religious daydreaming. Letting go of our character defects requires that we be willing to take the opposite action of the way we would act in the character defect. We reverse course, acting as if God has given us all that we need. This is called *repenting* in religious terms. If we want to be like Jesus, *acting as if* we are already becoming like Jesus is a great place to start. Over time, our honest and obedient actions will begin to change the way we think. If we want our life to change, we have to change the way we live it.

Millie Ann's Story

"The LORD directs the steps of the godly. He delights in every detail of their lives. Though they stumble, they will never fall, for the LORD holds them by the hand."

> Psalm 37:23,24 *NLT*

"As you discover your faults and sins, make no effort in your own strength to overcome them. This is a waste of time! Rather, abandon yourself immediately to God. Only He is able to destroy in you all that displeases Him."

> - Jeanne Guyon

We humbly asked Him to remove our shortcomings.

It seems like I make the best discoveries when I am going through the toughest times. As a result of one particular issue that has repeatedly brought tough times to me, I've come to realize how God can help me to better deal with all of the difficulties that I suffer.

For years I had been working myself into a frenzy over my inability to handle my finances. Now I want you to know that I make a good income and I have always known that there is no good reason for me to run out of money. However, time after time I would overspend and have to borrow money to make ends meet. This happened numerous times and every time I would end up in great despair, feeling isolated and hopeless about ever overcoming my bad habits and problems related to money. I can't count how many times I promised to do better and to change, but the harder I tried, the worse things got for me. Each day I was feeling more inadequate. I seriously doubted my ability to manage my own life. I was becoming ever more desperate.

Then one day, when I was quietly considering my situation, I realized that I was dealing with a very serious character defect. I had never thought of my problem in this way before. I had always thought that I could solve this problem as long as I worked hard enough or was smart enough. But when I started to think of my problem in terms of a character defect, I realized that I could never solve this problem on my own. It was, at the very least, bigger than me. I knew that I had to turn myself over to God in a more profound and personal way, otherwise this character defect would continue to rule me, ultimately destroying my and my daughter's future.

My sponsor from AA led to me Christ when I was about six months sober. While I had grown up attending church with my family, I had never known Christ as anything more than someone the priest talked about at Mass. The Christ I came to know by way of my sponsor was someone who had an interest in me and someone who I believed would want to be with me all of the time. Now, in turning over this most desperate problem that lived so deep within me, I felt like I wanted Christ to move into me in an ever deeper way in order to get rid of this deeply-rooted character defect. Later that same day I went into my bedroom and I got down on my knees beside my bed and prayed (pleading and begging was more like it) for Christ to take away this horribly defective part of my character. As I prayed I began to experience a very quiet sense of relief. Obviously nothing had changed in that moment except for maybe me. I knew that I did not have to bear this burden by myself anymore. I knew that God was going to be with me and He was going to help me. This made a world of difference.

Over the next few weeks I began to think a little differently about my problem. I began to see money differently, too. I realized that I had always been afraid of the responsibility of money and I had always been scared of success. Not wanting to be scared anymore, I started to look around for someone who could help me learn to better manage my income and finances. Remembering that someone once told me that prayer without action is a waste of time, I enrolled in a credit counseling program that was free of charge. The people at this program helped me to develop a budget that was workable, one that did not put my back up to the wall. I made no promises to anyone, not even to myself. My only commitment was to continue to surrender my character defect and my fear to God and to act in accordance with the guidance given to me by my credit counselor. It took over two years, but I finally got all of my credit cards paid off and I have begun saving money in the hopes of buying a home for me and my daughter.

My life is now marked by an increasing number of surrenders. Most are more subtle than the surrender I made over money. I have gained a greater appreciation for Christ, and I believe more strongly than ever in His love and compassion for me.

Life for me is far from perfect. I am, after all, a single mother who spent much of her life living wrongly, and there are still consequences for my failures. But, right in the midst of the hardships of my life, I know that the power of God is always available to me as long as I ask Him for His help and I surrender my will to His.

Step Eight

*We made a list of all persons we had harmed,
and became willing to make amends to them all.*

Step Eight is an exercise that helps heal the relationships that have been damaged by our addictions and self-centeredness. If we want to continue to grow in our life, we have to be willing to help others recover from the damage that we have caused them. The Step Eight process will not only help others recover from hurts and wounds; it will at the same time help us recover from the damage and the negative consequences that we've brought on ourselves.

Step Eight assumes and implies that we carry hidden within us a burden of guilt and shame for virtually every incident where we have hurt others, rejected others or ignored the needs of others. Step Eight is an exercise *and* an opportunity through which we can begin to set right the wrongs that we have done. Doing this will help lighten the burden of guilt and shame that we have carried alone for too long.

Step Eight continues and expands the shame-reducing process that we began in Step Four and Step Five. Simply admitting our wrongdoing and shortcomings is not enough in the relational and reciprocal world that we live in. We must be willing to get specific about how we have affected the lives of others, and we must be willing to take effective action in order to make things right. We must do this, otherwise we will continue living in the social alienation our addictions have created—the isolation that so easily fosters and fuels our addictions all the more. Isolation kills people who have addictions.

The Responsibility of Life

"Do to others as you would like them to do to you."
　　Luke 6:31 *NLT*

"We make good actions and let those actions speak for us."
　　- The Men of Operation Integrity

We made a list of all persons we had harmed, and became willing to make amends to them all.

We started to identify our shortcomings, all of which stem from our self-centeredness, in our Step Four inventory. We realized that we had lived for ourselves (usually without realizing it), and other people have suffered because of it. Now, because of God's power to transform us, things can be different. The recovery that we are experiencing today brings with it an increasing awareness of our shortcomings, which further illuminates our need for God and deepens our desire for the kind of life that only God can give to us. We see ourselves and the world around us differently from the way we did before. We can have hopeful enthusiasm for our future. This new life that God is giving to us is good. It is better than anything we could have provided for ourselves. But, as good as we may feel about ourselves and our recovery, most of us—if we are willing to look deep enough to see it—still experience a deep, nagging sense that there is unfinished business that we need to tend to. This *new life in Christ* that we are receiving will be short-lived if we don't continue to grow away from our selfishness, or if we forget how we have negatively impacted the lives of others.

Everything we say and everything we do affects the lives of people around us. In ways that are big and small, and often in ways we don't even realize, all that we say engages other people, bringing reactions and consequences back to us. Like it or not, we make an impact on the world—good or bad—beginning first and foremost with those closest to us. It is impossible to escape the impact and influence that we have. The most honest questions we can ask ourselves are, What will be the result of our lives? What impact will we have? Will we be men and women of change, growth and integrity or will we live for ourselves, taking from and consuming the people and the world around us?

Names of people we hurt: **What we did to hurt them:**

The Fundamentals of Forgiveness

"Do not judge others, and you will not be judged. Do not condemn others, or it will all come back against you. Forgive others, and you will be forgiven. Give, and you will receive. Your gift will return to you in full—pressed down, shaken together to make room for more, running over, and poured into your lap. The amount you give will determine the amount you get back."
 Luke 6:37-38 *NLT*

"Forgiveness is the fragrance the violet sheds on the heel that has crushed it."
 - Anonymous

"For my part, I believe in the forgiveness of sin and the redemption of ignorance."
 - Adlai Stevenson

We made a list of all persons we had harmed, and became willing to make amends to them all.

One of the great miracles that we will experience in our Twelve Step recovery process is how God will meet us more than halfway. Throughout Scripture we are told that even our smallest commitments and efforts will be met and rewarded with a return that far exceeds what we have invested. What God gives us in our recovery efforts should really be considered more like a gift, because it is not based on the magnitude of our efforts, but more on the sincerity of our hearts that is expressed through our efforts. We can rest knowing that even our greatest failures will be turned into good things, if we have done them with a sincere heart that seeks to know God and the love that He gives.

One of the ways that God turns our failures into something good is by helping us, when we are willing, to let go of the anger and resentment that we have had. To the degree that we are willing to forgive those who have hurt us, we will be able to receive the forgiveness that God gives, especially the forgiveness that other people give us. For you see, healing damaged relationships— forgiveness—is a two-way street. We have to be willing to forgive before we will be ready to receive forgiveness. Forgiving and being forgiven is the fundamental footing that must be in place before we can build a life that is relationally solid. As we already know, we can't build a forgiven life by ourselves. We have to have help. We will need help from our sponsors and our counselors, because every situation will be different. Even as we grow, we will have blind spots in our thinking. We need an enlarged point of view in order to take the best course of action, and our sponsors and counselors will help us to gain this much needed increase in perspective.

There is no doubt that some of the people we need to make amends to have been guilty of hurting us, too. Once again, these are situations where we should consult with our sponsors and our counselors in order to know the best way to proceed. One thing we know for sure is that, in each and every case, we are called to forgive. Forgiveness is the ultimate of God's commands. It is the ultimate obedience, too. When we forgive others, we become willing to let them "off the hook" at the emotional and psychological level. God commands us to forgive so that we can live better ourselves. Forgiveness is an act of love not only for others, but most of all for ourselves. The people who have hurt us will hold us hostage forever as long as we are unwilling to let go of our anger and resentment. For some of us there have been circumstances where someone hurt us with a criminal act. In such cases we should refer to our advisors. Most certainly we must be willing to alert law enforcement to what we know. We do this in order to put a stop to the damage that was done to us and, more importantly, to take responsible action that will help protect others in the future. While it is a good thing to see a dangerous person held accountable for his crimes, this does not excuse us from the necessity of forgiving the offender at a personal and spiritual level. Forgiving someone for hurting us does not mean that we excuse their bad behavior, either.

Who do we need to forgive and why?

Forgiveness – The Way of Healthy Living

"Be kind and compassionate to one another, forgiving each other, just as in Christ God forgave you."
> Ephesians 4:32 *NIV*

"To err is human, to forgive is divine."
> - Alexander Pope

We made a list of all persons we had harmed, and became willing to make amends to them all.

Forgiveness brings us home to be with God, spiritually. Forgiveness is God's standard practice for healthy living, and where we live spiritually affects where we are emotionally and psychologically. This is why forgiveness is so important to our overall mental health. It is the framework of compassion and empathy upon which our future health is built. As we breathe in and breathe out forgiveness, we are inhaling and exhaling God's most life-giving antidote for sin and destruction. Why do we forgive others? Because God forgave us first. Why does God forgive us? He forgives us so we can have life. God knows that nothing is more important for our emotional, psychological and spiritual health than forgiveness, and nothing will help us to make the most of God's gift of forgiveness like forgiving ourselves.

Forgiving ourselves begins with understanding our own human frailties and shortcomings. This will help us to have a more compassionate perspective. After all, our addictions did make sense to us at the time that we were doing them, didn't they? God understands this, you see. He understands why we have done the things that we have done. He understands that, as silly and as stupid as our actions were, they somehow made sense to us at the time that we were doing them. God understands the insanity of addiction. He understands that while we are responsible for making good use of the help He provides, we are not completely at fault for all of our insane thinking. We don't know everything, and our decisions and thinking have suffered from faulty and misguided beliefs. Because of His complete and total understanding, He is willing to forgive us for the things we have done. For example, even when Christ was being crucified, He didn't hold anything against the people who were killing him. In Luke 23:34 Jesus, while being crucified, is quoted as saying, "Father, forgive these people for they don't know what they are doing." Our attitude should be the same. As God forgives us, we are called to forgive those who have hurt us. And this begins with a compassionate understanding of our own failures and addictions.

Many sponsors and counselors will encourage us to include our own names on the list we make of the people we have hurt. After all, no one has been more hurt by our addictions than we have. Unless we forgive ourselves, we will never fully enjoy the forgiveness that God and other people offer to us. Forgiving ourselves connects us more closely with God and the world around us. As we forgive ourselves, like God does, we will be better able to escape the resentment we have had for other people, for God and for ourselves. Self-forgiveness helps increase our appreciation for just how connected and interrelated to all of God's creation we are, in ways that we will never fully understand until we are with Christ in eternity. Forgiving ourselves helps us to participate with God's creation in healthy and dynamic ways, ways that will far exceed our greatest expectations and assumptions.

James and Bethe are a young married couple who had previously lived lives of addictive sexual immorality, until they made the decision to give their lives to God by pursuing an intimate relationship with Jesus Christ. Together, they began working a Twelve Step recovery program which included long-term counseling. Their counselor gave them an assignment to read some Christ-centered recovery literature, after which they wrote this statement:

We struggled to survive life for many years. Everyday we felt like victims because we had both been severely abused when we were children. But now, we don't think of ourselves as victims anymore. With God's help, a change is underway inside of us. We think differently than we used to think—our attitude is different.

We don't need to destroy ourselves or each other with anger and hate like we used to. We don't need to think thoughts of revenge anymore. God knows what has happened to us and He is in the process of making it all turn out good. He knows the truth. He will make the correct judgments and He will give mercy as He sees fit. We leave all of our hurts and mistakes in His hands.

We now know that God will not judge us for what happened to us, but we will be judged by how we live our lives and how we treat others. We are responsible for our actions. We are responsible for what we do with what we know. We have no power to change the past, but as God is our strength we can change our future.

So, we have decided to make the most of the opportunities to experience healing and growth. As we experience God's power working within us, we will pass this healing onto our children, our family and to others, even to those who have hurt us. The ripples of healing in the pond of our lives will spread throughout future generations."

- James and Bethe, 2007 - In recovery for 2 years

How have we hurt ourselves through self-resentment and self-destruction?

Making It Real

"My dear, dear friends, if God loved us like this, we certainly ought to love each other. No one has seen God, ever. But if we love one another, God dwells deeply within us, and his love becomes complete in us—perfect love!"

I John 4:11, 12 *The Message*

"A critical component of recovery is recognizing and admitting personal responsibility in relationships."
- Anonymous

We made a list of all persons we had harmed, and became willing to make amends to them all.

We waste our recovery efforts when we forget our failures. Forgetting our failures can lead us into the most self-centered and insidious of all sins, self-righteousness. With a short memory and a little complacency, we become piously religious, self-satisfied and woefully unaware of the difficult world that we've created for ourselves and others. This is why one of the most critical components of recovery is to recognize and admit our personal responsibility in our relationships. And, this is why it is so important for us to acknowledge the people that have been harmed by our selfish attitudes and actions. We must—for our own sakes and for theirs—see how they've been affected by us. The opportunity and possibility to recover from our addictions compels us to ask for forgiveness, to help those negatively impacted by our lives and—when it's available—accept reconciliation from them while forgiving others, so that we can all grow in freedom.

Let us set aside any remaining selfish or prideful motivations that we are aware of. Starting with our recovering fellowship, let us begin to make personal investments in others, working to expand and heal the world around us. Let us take this momentum of love to our families, to our communities, to our work places and to our churches. We want more today than to just have our lives and our circumstances improved. We want to see other people healed and their lives and circumstances improved, too. We are taking on new ways of thinking, new personalities, becoming more concerned with loving others and honoring them as people who've been created by God to know Him and His love.

Name some people who would benefit from a healthier expression of your love.

The Poison of Resentment

"For if you forgive men when they sin against you, your heavenly Father will also forgive you. But if you do not forgive men their sins, your Father will not forgive your sins."
> Matthew 6:14, 15 *NIV*

"Don't carry a grudge. While you're carrying the grudge, the other guy's out dancing."
> - Buddy Hackett

We made a list of all persons we had harmed, and became willing to make amends to them all.

It is very important that we keep our focus, remembering that we are working our own recovery program and not someone else's. Our faults are our responsibility, but the faults of others are not, nor are they our concern. Our recovery necessitates that we recognize that while others have accidentally and even sometimes intentionally harmed us, any resentments that we entertain against them will handicap us spiritually and emotionally. Resentment poisons our hearts. Then it circulates into every part of our lives. It's like taking poison and expecting someone else to get sick and die.

When we hold a grudge against someone else, we are actually bringing misery back onto ourselves. Resentment creates a kind of attitudinal foul odor that keeps others from getting close to us. Resentment can be intoxicating, and then we get hijacked by unhappiness, which further alienates us from others. But honestly recognizing the hurt others have done to us—and giving the offenders our undeserved forgiveness—will help to cleanse us from the stagnating resentment that will destroy us. Allowing others the freedom to be wrong helps us to see life—most notably our own life—more clearly. We will be better able to objectively acknowledge and embrace our shortcomings as well as our strengths.

Thinking and living this way is a relational kind of humility that frees us to receive God's strength coming to us through the holes that our weaknesses create, resulting in an increased freedom to love other people without barriers. As we learn to care for others, both the good and the bad, we learn to better care for ourselves with increasing aptitude and insight as a child of God. Forgiving others and being forgiven go hand in hand. We can't have one without the other.

List those who have harmed you and who you need to make amends to.

Recovery is a Gift but it is Not Free

"Therefore, if you are offering your gift at the altar and there remember that your brother has something against you, leave your gift there in front of the altar. First go and be reconciled to your brother; then come and offer your gift."

> Matthew 5:23, 24 NIV

"Our privileges can be no greater than our obligations. The protection of our rights can endure no longer than the performance of our responsibilities."

> - John F. Kennedy

We made a list of all persons we had harmed, and became willing to make amends to them all.

The kind of work that we do in our recovery program helps us better recognize the work of God in our lives. We can now begin to see that we have been made for supernatural purposes and that it is possible for us to fulfill the destiny that God has planned for us.

God created us with a plan. He has divine purposes in mind. As we prepare ourselves to make amends, God is preparing us to pass on to others some of the goodness that He has given us. Our life, addiction and recovery is all part of God's plan. He is the master creator who specializes in bringing goodness out of tragedy. This is what our Step Eight recovery work is all about—turning bad into good. We are now ready to begin directing goodness into the lives of others, where before it had been directed into our own lives. Our personality, our talent and our charm will never be enough to do this. We will have to have God's help, and He will be sure to give it to us. Our friends and loved ones need a love that is not based on who we are. They need a love based on who we are created for. Any attempts that we make by our own power alone—no matter how great, sincere or committed—will inevitably become little more than co-dependency without the connection of real love, which comes only from God.

The power to love and live well is a gift from God, and it comes with profound spiritual and social responsibilities. God provides the power but we are totally involved; the part we play is indispensable. Our place in the universe begins to make sense as we figure this out. As we develop authentic, God-centered relationships, we become whole and well-balanced human beings that are able to live out our responsibilities and fully enjoy the pleasure of giving and receiving.

Our job and responsibility at this point in time is to make a list of the people whom we have hurt. There are no excuses—no ifs, ands, or buts. Excuses, procrastination and delay for any reason are understandable, but unacceptable. Excuses stop our recovery dead in its tracks. There is no reason to delay.

List more names of people we have harmed.

Moving Forward, Back into Relationship

"Be strong and courageous. Do not be afraid or terrified because of them, for the Lord your God goes with you; he will never leave you nor forsake you."

Deuteronomy 31:6 NIV

"Until you conquer the fear of being an outsider, an outsider you will remain."

- C.S. Lewis

We made a list of all persons we had harmed, and became willing to make amends to them all.

We are going to make more and more amazing discoveries as we continue to make a list of the people we have harmed. One of these discoveries will be realizing how incredible it is that there is anyone who loves us at all, considering the way that we have treated others in the past. However, at the same time—as we face the facts of our self-centeredness in more realistic ways—we will also learn that we have always been loved far more than we could ever understand, because of God and the love He has shown to us. Recognizing our depraved nature in contrast to God's forgiving love enlightens us to a new way of thinking and operating. Fear becomes displaced by courage. Our relationships are affected for the better. We can positively relate with others today in ways that would have been impossible before because of our fear of being hurt and rejected. But, there is a new kind of power inside of us now. The life we live is no longer our own. God, through His love, has taken us over.

Following through with the change that is happening inside of us, we begin to treat people differently, respectfully. The first thing we must do to make amends to others is to stop hurting them. In the past we treated others the way they treated us, but now we will treat others the way God has treated us— respectfully, whether they deserve it or not.

What others do to us and how they treat us is much less important now. We hope that others will give us love and respect—but if they don't, we won't need to get upset, retaliate or fall into self-pity anymore. Our desire is to simply love others with the same love that we have received from God and others. We don't have to manufacture this love; we just pass it along. We share what we have been given. Thinking in this way helps us to set aside our fears of rejection; then we will be able to do for others what God, our sponsors and our counselors have done for us.

Motivated by the love we have discovered, coupled with the commitment to change the generational patterns that our families have developed, we set some boundaries for ourselves and we accept boundaries that others place on us. Then, we take these next steps forward. First, we became willing to make amends to those we hurt—unconditionally. Second, we became willing to recognize and accept healthy limitations and to make *"living amends"* by the way that we relate to others in the future. Hopefully we have learned not to profess our "good intentions." We don't make promises, especially promises that we cannot guarantee. Instead, let us make good actions and let those actions speak for us.

If we ever refuse an opportunity to make a wrong right, we shut the doors and windows of the spiritual home that God is building within us. Nothing gets in and nothing gets out. Darkness begins to close in and we miss the leading of God's Spirit. Then, without the benefit of God's Spirit leading us, we inevitably create more of the chaos that we are trying to avoid.

So, let us take what we have learned and move it from our head to our heart, and from our heart to our feet, where relationships are renewed step-by- step. With our feet of action placed firmly on God and a supportive recovery fellowship, we will find the stability that we need to make our lives—and the lives of others—change for the better. Everybody wins!

Step Nine

We made direct amends to such people wherever possible, except when to do so would injure them or others.

Step Nine is an effective and proven way for us to set aside old hurts and move toward a healthier life and healthier relationships. At first it may seem like Step Nine is a very one-sided experience because we are the ones who take the initiative in Step Nine, but it is not. Everyone, you see, is benefited when we make amends for our wrongs. Doing so brings healing to everyone involved, starting with ourselves.

Step Nine is about opportunities and possibilities, not guarantees. Our job is to simply make good use of the opportunities that are available to us. As we do this, it becomes possible for our fractured and broken relationships to be healed, to become new and better than ever before. At the same time, it is important that we recognize that we may never be able to repair all of the damage and hurts that we have caused. And, we also need to understand that our apologies alone will never be enough to make things right. We cannot earn our way back into the lives of others anymore than we can earn our salvation from God. God and others are in control here. There are no guarantees. The only thing we have any control over is our attitude and our actions. We can only do what we can do, and we need to be willing to trust God for the results.

Talk is Cheap

"God blesses those who work for peace, for they will be called the children of God."
  Matthew 5:9 *NLT*

"Let's not talk prudence while practicing evasion."
  - Alcoholics Anonymous

We made direct amends to such people wherever possible, except when to do so would injure them or others.

It is time that we begin repairing the damage and hurt that we have caused other people, whenever and wherever it is possible for us to do so. Initiating peace and healing will always be one of the responsibilities that we have in the life that God is giving to us. So, let us commit ourselves to helping others recover from the pain that we have caused them—pain that they didn't create or deserve.

This will probably not be easy. Ask any recovering addict that has preceded us in the process of making Step Nine amends and they will tell you that making amends is hard work. And it is all the more difficult when we are offering our amends to people who, in all likelihood, may resent us. Unfortunately, there is no shortcut or magic wand in setting our wrongs right, especially where other people are involved. Looking for shortcuts will only get us lost in our own self-created world of fantasy and make-believe. Recovery from addiction and enjoying healthy relationships only happens in the real world. If we really want to recover and have good relationships in the future, we will have to be willing to live in the real world.

Making amends is not optional if we want to recover, grow and change. The best thing we can do is to help those who have been hurt by our addictions and the self-centered ways that we have lived our lives.

Feeling and Doing

"This is the kind of life you've been invited into, the kind of life Christ lived. He suffered everything that came his way so you would know that it could be done, and also know how to do it, step by step. He never did one thing wrong, Not once said anything amiss.
They called him every name in the book and he said nothing back."

> I Peter 2:21–23 *The Message*

"It is not until we love a person in all his ugliness that we can make him beautiful, or ourselves either."

> - Frederick Buechner

We made direct amends to such people wherever possible, except when to do so would injure them or others.

Let's be honest about the deep anger and resentment that we have held against some of the people to whom we owe amends. All of us have suffered to some degree because of the anger we have stored up on the inside. If we take a moment to honestly consider this, we will see that there is really no question that we have felt this way. Anger and resentment are some of the core feelings that drive our addictions. The only real relevant question now is, Can we—*will* we— face our anger honestly, with integrity, and not let it stand in the way of our recovery?

Recovery and future growth will not allow us to sidestep our feelings. We have to be willing to confront the destructive feelings that we have felt for certain specific people (this may even include a group of people or a particular demographic) if we want to recover and make healthy changes to our relationships in the future. Feeling the way we feel does not excuse us from taking the important steps that we need to take to make amends to the people we have harmed. Feelings are feelings and nothing more. They are like lights on the dashboard of our lives. They tell us about important things that are going on under the hood but they are not intended to dictate the actions we take, nor do they excuse our procrastinations.

There may be times when we realize that some of the people who are on our amends list have caused us harm, and the wrongs they've done to us far exceed anything we've done to them. It is vitally important that we keep our focus here. The wrongs that other people have done to us are not our concern at this point in time. We need to make the decision to no longer hold their wrongs against them. After consulting with our advisors, let us contact these people and apologize to them for our inappropriate actions, offering to do whatever we can do to repair the damage we have caused. These particular people may have never acknowledged the hurt and pain they have caused us, and maybe they never will. Nevertheless, let us continue to forgive them everyday, not because they are innocent or because they deserve forgiveness, but because we need to do so in order to continue to recover from our addictions *and* to heal from the damage they did to us.

Occasionally feelings of anger and resentment will return. Because of this, we should diligently monitor our own thoughts and feelings and be willing to let go of any renewed anger that comes up. While we may not have a future relationship with these particular people, our attitude toward them, ourselves and others will be radically improved only to the degree that we are willing to forgive them and make amends to them. We can be honest about how things really were in our past relationships. We don't need to make excuses for our friends, our families or for ourselves anymore. Things simply were the way they were, and today they are the way they are. We can hope and even pray that someday things may change, that we can have a healthy and happy relationship with all people and that all people will recognize that our new life and values are worth appreciating. But, in order for us to continue to grow in God's plan for our lives, we must remember that other people's attitudes toward us are none of our business. It is between them and God.

True Forgiveness

"Put yourself aside, and help others get ahead. Don't be obsessed with getting your own advantage. Forget yourselves long enough to lend a helping hand."

Philippians 2:3 *The Message*

"The people who gave you the consequences are not your enemies. By seeing those who give you consequences as the enemy, you keep yourself stuck in justifying your behavior. Your real problem is your denial and self–delusion."

- Patrick Carnes, Ph.D

We made direct amends to such people wherever possible, except when to do so would injure them or others.

True forgiveness is something that we can give and something we can receive, but we can never force it on others or demand it from others. Forgiveness does not condone, excuse or minimize wrongdoing. Forgiving simply means to look directly at the wrongdoer—knowing full well the destructive impact of their actions—recognize them for who they are and what they have done, and then offer to them a mercy and grace that is completely undeserved.

The giving and receiving of forgiveness is an act of humility. When we forgive, we see others—even the most disturbed—with a kind of empathy that is fundamental to our deepest humanity. It is the way God created us to be. With empathy and forgiveness, we see others as people whom God loves. We see them as people God wants to be close to. We honor God by seeing the people He created—no matter how undeserving they are—as worthy of love and respect. This doesn't mean that forgiveness guarantees that all of our relationships will go back to the way they were before. Forgiveness, after all, does not excuse inexcusable acts. It sees the facts and sets healthy parameters for the future. This is needed for both the offender and the victim to move forward and live a better life in the future.

We need to be careful not to ask for forgiveness when what we really want is to be excused for our wrongdoing. Wrongdoing is never an accident. Accidents can be excused, but selfish people that do selfish things need forgiveness. Asking for forgiveness is an act of repentance as well as an act of confession. Repentance doesn't debate; it never bargains or rationalizes. Confession makes no claim, nor does it minimize or argue. We are not here, after all, to make excuses. We are here to make a simple request for undeserved mercy. We should never dispute the facts when confronted about wrongdoing we have done. Let the criticisms and the charges be what they are. We are responsible for the way that we forgive others. How other people forgive us is their business, not ours. We may never again experience the same respect and freedom we had before. We may never again enjoy the unmitigated trust of our families. Other people will invariably adjust to how they relate to us in the future. The boundaries that they impose on us are a direct result of the pain and hurt we have caused them. Being committed to love others unconditionally, we should accept these limitations, committing ourselves to respect the lives of others in the same way that we would like to be respected.

If we struggle to forgive others, we should pray for those who have hurt us or let us down. Prayer helps us to overcome the resentments that inhibit our emotional growth. We should pray, asking that God will give both our enemies and our loved ones hope for their life, help for their difficulties, grace for their struggles, and the courage to live abundantly. We should pray for our enemies in the same way that we pray for ourselves.

An Addict Speaks to His Family

"What this adds up to, then, is this: no more lies, no more pretense. Tell your neighbor the truth. In Christ's body we're all connected to each other, after all. When you lie to others, you end up lying to yourself. Go ahead and be angry. You do well to be angry--but don't use your anger as fuel for revenge. And don't stay angry. Don't go to bed angry. Don't give the Devil that kind of foothold in your life. Did you use to make ends meet by stealing? Well, no more! Get an honest job so that you can help others who can't work."

Ephesians 4:25-28 *The Message*

"It is not possible to love others unless our hearts are growing in faith and hope. Faith and hope birth love as we live out our calling in anticipation of his coming."

- Dan Allender, Ph.D

We made direct amends to such people wherever possible, except when to do so would injure them or others.

The following is adapted from Al-Anon literature. Al-Anon, a sister organization to Alcoholics Anonymous, helps those closely related to alcoholics and drug addicts recover from the negative effects addiction has had on them. Al-Anon emphasizes how honest and open family dialogue can promote the healing process.

Dear Loved Ones

I recognize and admit that I am addicted. And I know I need your help. Please, don't scold or lecture me. Verbal attacks only reinforce my self-loathing and self-hatred, and I hate myself enough already. Please do your best not to be angry with me. I doubt you would be angry at me for being a diabetic. Addiction is a kind of disease too.

Don't let your love for me, or the anxiety my actions create, cause you to do what I need to do for myself. When you take on my responsibilities, my failure to assume them is encouraged all the more. My feelings of guilt will increase and you will likely feel even more resentful against me. Don't accept my problems or excuses because I am inclined to promise anything to appease you and others. The very the nature of my addiction makes it difficult for me to keep my promises, even though I do have good intentions most of the time.

Don't make threats you are not willing to carry out. Once you make a decision, stick to it. Don't believe everything I tell you; you know I have lied in the past and I will likely do it again. Denying reality is common with addicts like me. And we typically lose respect for those who we can fool easily. Don't let me take advantage of you or exploit you. Real love is possible only with decency and fair play in relationships. Don't cover up for me, or spare me the consequences of my destructive behavior. Don't pay my bills or meet my obligations. Doing this will probably reduce or postpone the very crisis that would compel me to get the help I need. And I can only deny my problem as long as you, and others, provide an easy escape from the inevitable consequences of my addictive acting out.

Above all, please learn everything you can about addiction, because we are all addicted in one way or another. Go to open recovery meetings and listen to recovering addicts whenever you can. Attend your own codependency recovery meetings as often as possible. Read the literature, and keep in touch with others in recovery. They're the people who can best help you see our addicted relationship clearly.

I love you,
Your Recovering Addict

Actions Speak Louder than Words

"This is how I want you to conduct yourself in these matters. If you enter your place of worship and, about to make an offering, you suddenly remember a grudge a friend has against you, abandon your offering, leave immediately, go to this friend and make things right. Then and only then, come back and work things out with God."
    Matthew 5:24 *The Message*

"If you want to lift yourself up, lift someone else up."
    - Booker T. Washington

We made direct amends to such people wherever possible, except when to do so would injure them or others.

As we start to make our amends, we should make every attempt to offer ourselves to others in a sensitive and thoughtful way. We need to deeply consider the thoughts and feelings of others. Let us make the commitment to speak wholehearted words of grace and compassion. Where in the past we have shown disregard and selfishness, today let us reflect the image of God's love. In recovery and making amends, it is our job to honor others and to give back to them what we have taken away. We should acknowledge to others that they never deserved to be treated the way we treated them. They deserved better. It is vitally important that we come right out and tell them that we want to make things right and that our restitution begins with a change in our attitude toward them, reflected by the way we interact with them in the future. Our message is simple: Today we see things differently. We are less important; God and other people are more important.

There may be times when we feel like people are out to get us. Maybe they are and maybe they aren't. We are, after all, not the only ones who are susceptible to resentment and who sometimes want revenge. When we are willing to be open-minded about the attacks we perceive from others, it's likely that we will see that these attacks were aimed at our addictive thinking, our selfish actions and our sin, not really at us. So, when we feel attacked, let's do our best not to defend ourselves. If we have done something to warrant an attack from another person, we can apologize and ask what we can do to make things right. Then, above all else, let us change our actions. Actions really do speak louder than words.

Building healthier relationships with others requires that we address the ways that we have harmed ourselves, and as we begin to make amends to ourselves, we will begin to create the necessary spiritual momentum that helps to move us forward in making amends to others. Many of us needed to make changes in our eating and exercise habits—or lack thereof. When we had hurt ourselves financially, we faced it and with the help of our sponsors and counselors, we made the changes that were necessary for us to begin developing financial integrity. When we had hurt ourselves emotionally, we talked it over with others. Sometimes we even wrote ourselves letters, addressing them to ourselves at specific ages from our childhood. Sometimes, sitting in front of a mirror, we privately read these letters to ourselves. We always read these letters to our sponsors, to our counselors and even to some of the people in our recovering fellowship. Following the example of others, we learned to give ourselves grace and understanding because we realize now that no one has it all together except for Jesus.

Recovery is not a straight line from Point A to Point Z. No matter how good or how bad things get, one thing is for sure: things are going to change.

Proceed with Caution

"I tell you, love your enemies. Help and give without expecting a return. You'll never – I promise - regret it. Live out this God-created identity the way our Father lives toward us, generously and graciously, even when we're at our worst. Our Father is kind; you be kind."
    Luke 6:35-36 *The Message*

"The love of our neighbor in all its fullness simply means being able to say to him, 'What are you going through?'"
    - Simone Weil

We made direct amends to such people wherever possible, except when to do so would injure them or others.

Most of our lives have been spent in a ditch of selfishness alongside the road of life. As we move forward, trying to get our life back on track, it is critical that we maintain a balanced perspective. It is very easy to overcorrect and end up in another ditch where we obsessively think that we have to right every wrong perfectly. This kind of perfectionistic thinking will hurt us. It is fanciful, make-believe, and it will stand in the way of our relationship with God. Perfectionistic thinking is of the devil. Even God—while He is perfect—is not a perfectionist, and we should not be either. Having a balanced point of view that recognizes both our responsibilities and our limitations will help us to make rational decisions and find workable solutions as we make our amends.

There will be times where it's impossible for us to make amends because we simply do not have the internal fortitude that we need. There will also be situations where we lack the resources or the opportunity we need, so we will have to defer our efforts to another time. And, there will be situations where approaching certain people is not a wise thing to do because we may do more harm than good.

We need to be careful when contacting anyone that we have had inappropriate sexual relationships with, or when contacting anyone who has acted out our addictions with us. Old acquaintances, with no ill will, can easily derail us and we can derail them, too. In light of this fact, it is essential that we keep ourselves away from situations where we may relapse and lose the freedom that we have worked so hard to gain. In addition to this, we must be vigilant to avoid situations where our best intentions may create more hurt and harm to other people, especially to the innocent bystanders that are close to us and to those whom we have hurt. If God wants us to see former lovers and acquaintances, He will arrange for us to meet them in a way where we can all be safe. We should ask our sponsors and our counselors what they think regarding these situations. They will have good advice for us as to how we can safely and reasonably make these most difficult amends.

While it may not be wise for us to contact certain people directly, we can begin to make amends to them by assisting other people who essentially represent them in some way. Changing our attitude towards people in general— especially to those to whom we are sexually attracted—and giving all kinds of people appropriate and dignified respect, is a great beginning. Making amends to former lovers and to people that we have objectified is vital for us to increase the integrity that has taken root in us. Letting go of titillating fantasies or memories of sexual conquest is a great place to start in making these kinds of amends. And we also must be willing to give up the notion that we need others to meet our needs— financially, socially, relationally or romantically. Making amends requires that we stop seeing others as objects for pleasure, protection or provision. People belong to God, not to us. Making amends requires that we redirect our memories and see the past with realistic clarity. Doing this will help change the way we think. One way to do this is to pray for those whom we've held hostage in our fantasies and memories. We just let go of our lusts, sexual or otherwise. This pays off for us in a big way because praying for others changes us at the most fundamental level of our mind and our emotions. Prayer, over time, changes the way that we see others and ourselves. As we pray for others, let us pray for their health, their safety and their happiness, praying that they would experience the fulfillment of their hopes and dreams and, more importantly, come to a place where they experience the ever-increasing power of God's love.

As we are willing to change the way we think and act, we will develop healthier ways of responding to the thoughts, the memories and the varying stimulations that have driven our addictive and destructive impulses in the past. And as we make amends to others, we will see a positive change in our current and future relationships.

Life Liberated

"Pay all your debts, except the debt of love for others. You can never finish paying that! If you love your neighbor, you will fulfill all the requirements of God's law."

Romans 13:8 *NIV*

"Honest men fear neither the light nor the dark."

- Thomas Fuller, M.D.

We made direct amends to such people wherever possible, except when to do so would injure them or others.

Learning to love ourselves the way that God loves us will give us an ever- increasing freedom to live our lives. This freedom to live is not just a freedom from our addictions; it is a fully liberated life that begins on the inside of us and then moves out into all of the ways that we express ourselves. The liberty that God gives is not subject to the limitations and demands that we experience in our day-to-day lives, and while this freedom is bigger than our everyday lives, it does not make us immune to feeling fear when we are faced with uncertainty. God gives the kind of freedom and liberty that empowers and equips us to act with courage even in the face of uncertainty, when we feel fear. And, in the same way, we may feel pain but we can act with kindness even when feeling pain. The gift and responsibility of freedom is most evident when we address the negative consequences we've created, and when we make amends to those who have been hurt by the way we've lived in the past. When speaking with those to whom we owe amends, we will want to share with them that we recognize that we have had an addiction, that we know that our past actions have been hurtful, and that we want to make things right to the best of our ability. Sharing the facts of our addictions and our mistakes in *a general way* allows us to communicate with others from a standpoint of humility and honesty. We don't have to share every gory and ugly detail with them. We don't need to air out all of our dirty laundry, either. This is not about the past; it is about the present and about the future. We should only share what will be helpful to them and to others. Being forthright in this way, we begin to establish healthier communication with those that we've hurt. It will also help to put them at ease, and it will put us in a place where we can more effectively make the amends that we need to make. Sharing in this way will also open the door for others to honestly share their feelings with us. Dialogue must be an honest two-way street. We must be willing to listen—honestly and openly listen—in order to understand how we have hurt them and what we need to do to help them.

Some amends can and should be made face-to-face. Some can never be made directly. Others will have to be postponed for a better time. We'll be of little benefit to anyone if, in our attempts to clear our own conscience, we offer ourselves as sacrificial lambs. We should consult with our sponsors and our counselors about situations where we face serious consequences. We never want to run away from the reality of our past mistakes, but we also do not want to be shortsighted, disregarding our current relationships or responsibilities in an attempt to be a hero to the past. Our sponsors and counselors help us to know how to handle each situation. When we face situations where people demand certain answers from us that we do not want to give, we consult with our sponsors and counselors. Sometimes a three-way meeting between us, our victim and our counselors is necessary for things to get going in the right direction.

There is rarely a good reason to hurry. It is far better to do recovery well than to do it fast!

Step Ten

We continued to take personal inventory and when we were wrong, promptly admitted it.

Step Ten marks a shift in the focus of our recovery program. It is the first of what can be considered—along with Steps Eleven and Twelve—*the maintenance steps*. This is where we move past the heavy lifting of Steps Four through Nine and on to a maintenance program that will enable us to continuously receive God's transforming grace.

Step Ten is about developing ongoing day-to-day habits and a lifestyle where we continuously monitor our thoughts, our feelings and our actions in order to recognize when we are drifting away from God's purpose and plan for our lives. Step Ten is about vigilance; it is about making consistent changes that help keep our lives balanced on the beam of God's loving purpose and plan.

Step Ten is about more than just staying "sober," although staying sober will always be an important concern for all of us. This step is about maintaining healthy and balanced lives according to God's directions, so that we can reliably bring goodness to the people that God brings our way. We must be willing to make honest self-searching a regular, disciplined part of our day if we are going to make the most of our lives. Until we are willing to consistently recognize and admit the wrongs that still lurk within us, and unless we persistently make healthy changes in our thinking and living, we will not be able to consistently experience the joy that God has to give us, nor will we have the persistence to give God's goodness to others.

Integrity Inside and Out

"God is in charge of human life, watching and examining us from the inside and out.
> Proverbs 20:27 *The Message*

"The genesis of an obedient life is our confession; most notably the confession of our disobedience is what prompts us to live an obedient life with God."
> - Ann Lamott

We continued to take personal inventory and when we were wrong, promptly admitted it.

Ever notice how easy it is to become more concerned with how we look on the outside than with the honest reality of our inner character? It's not like we intend to be dishonest, because we don't. We want and intend to live right and to do good but—inevitably it seems—we slip off the path of God's leading when we become overly concerned with how we look to others. Then, the failures that follow make us feel embarrassed and ashamed so we naturally—instinctively—cover up and hide the failure and powerlessness that we don't want others to see.

Trying to act good on the outside in order to show that we are good on the inside sets us up for failure. It adds to our dysfunctional way of thinking and living. We think and feel one way, but then we act out in other ways—ways that are contrary to what we know to be right. And when our actions go against our true convictions, we get split into pieces spiritually and psychologically. This results in a kind of deep interpersonal disintegration that, sadly, we will probably not even realize is happening to us. Just like with our primary addiction, the only way to break this cycle of denial and disintegration is to admit that we have a problem. Specifically, we have to be willing to admit that we suffer from the great obsession that all human beings—with the exception of Jesus—

seem to suffer from: we want to be bigger and more powerful than we really are.

To address this kind of deep-rooted sinfulness effectively, we have to admit that we are obsessed with getting our act together so that others will be impressed with us and our efforts. We must admit our struggles if we want to be free from them. This even includes admitting how obsessed we have been to overcome our struggles. We need to admit that we don't have our act together and that we never *did* have our act together. We need to accept in our innermost selves that, even if it were possible for us to get our act together, all that we would ever have would be nothing more than an act.

The first act of integrity is to recognize and admit how we lack integrity.

A Lifestyle of Vigilance

"So let's not allow ourselves to get fatigued doing good. At the right time we will harvest a good crop if we don't give up, or quit. Right now, therefore, every time we get the chance, let us work for the benefit of all, starting with the people closest to us in the community of faith."
Galatians 6:9 -10 *The Message*

"If the Spirit of God detects anything in you that is wrong, He does not ask you to put it right; He asks you to accept the light, and He will put it right. A child of the light confesses instantly and stands bared before God; a child of the darkness says – "Oh, I can explain that away." When once the light breaks and the conviction of wrong comes, be a child of the light, and confess, and God will deal with what is wrong; if you vindicate yourself, you prove yourself to be a child of the darkness."
- Oswald Chambers

We continued to take personal inventory and when we were wrong, promptly admitted it.

We must never forget that we are powerless over our addictions and that our lives are beyond our ability to manage on our own. We also need to remember that we have come to believe that we can recover from our addictions because we have encountered other people who are recovering from their addictions. Then, wanting to survive our addictions and live, we made the decision to trust God with our lives the best we knew how, while at the same time we recognized that our trust in Him and our relationship with Him needed to include trusting the people that God brought along to help us.

As our trust in God and other people grows, we begin to admit to ourselves, to God and to certain trustworthy people who we really are, what we think about ourselves and how we feel about the world around us. We realize that we cannot get rid of our character defects on our own and that the only worthwhile thing to do is to ask God to remove our character defects from us. Then, as our character defects weaken over time, we become more aware of how we have hurt others in the past. By offering our apologies and assistance to those that we have hurt and by forgiving those who have hurt us, we accomplish something that no one else can ever do. No one can make our amends or our apologies for us. Doing this work ourselves is a very effective part of healing and integrating our hearts and our minds together as one.

The growth we experience motivates us to continue on. Maintaining a trusting relationship with God while at the same time considering other people as more important than ourselves, helps insure that we will continue to grow away from our addictions. A lifestyle of obedience to God draws us, step-by-step, on a continuing journey where our faith is increased and our hopefulness is expanded. We begin to see a new character form within us and a new life take shape ahead of us. But we won't stop now. We can't stop now because there is no middle road in recovery. We continue to grow, or our addictions will begin to overtake us once again. It is critical that we recognize that even the most subtle of our thoughts and our feelings lead to action, in one way or the other, good or bad. We never just stay the same. Complacency puts us at risk of losing ourselves to our own addictions once again. So, it is critical that we know what is going on inside of us. We must be willing to surrender our counterfeit appearances, even at the most personal and fundamental level. Our future requires that we have an honest grasp of who we really are; it requires that we prefer God's plan more than our own.

What benefit do we gain, or what good can we offer if we abandon our recovery incomplete?

A Breakthrough for Gary and His Family

"Don't be so naive and self-confident. You're not exempt. You could fall flat on your face as easily as anyone else. Forget about self-confidence; it's useless. Cultivate God-confidence."

    1 Corinthians 10:12 *The Message*

"The power to honor the truth – to speak it and be it – is at the heart of true masculinity."

    - Leanne Payne

We continued to take personal inventory and when we were wrong, promptly admitted it.

I began my personal Twelve Step recovery program about three years ago as a way to get a grip on my workaholism. For years my wife had been bugging me about not being home enough. She also complained that when I was at home, I was "not really there." It wasn't until I was in my early fifties and facing divorce and the loss of my family that I started to take her seriously. So, my wife and I went to see our local pastor and he suggested that I had a problem with my attitude and priorities about my work. (I thought he was full of BS.) He also suggested that I meet with a professional counselor who told me flat-out that he thought I was addicted to my work. (Bummer, I thought. I love my work.)

Fearing that my wife would leave and take the kids, I joined the men's recovery group at my church and slowly I began to see that I really was addicted to work. I realized this not because of the ridiculously long hours I put in but because I was doing my work for all the wrong reasons. I was more than passionate about my work. It was how I defined myself. The only way I thought of myself was in relationship to work. If work was good, I was good. If work was bad, I would feel like everything in life was bad. No matter how I sliced and diced it, I knew that I was a workaholic.

Following the guidance I got from the recovery group, I enlisted the help of a man who had been a longtime participant in the group. He is a recovering alcoholic and seemed to know what recovery was all about. I asked him to help me do the Twelve Steps and he agreed. We become close friends as he helped me work the steps for myself. While I was doing my recovery program, I continued to see the same counselor about once a month.

When I got to Step Ten, my sponsor suggested that I spend a month keeping an ongoing journal of my days, noting my schedule, my activities, my thoughts and my feelings. This seemed like a strange thing to do but I knew that my sponsor had done it for himself years before, and when I discussed it with my counselor he thought it was a good idea too. So, not being quite sure of what this was all about, I began to keep an ongoing journal that inventoried my life in real time. It was like recording my life while my life was taking place.

Much of my work responsibility has to do with travel. I am all over the country, spending 10-15 days a month away from home. Occasionally, but not very often, I will succumb to the temptation to look at an adult movie at the hotels I stay in. I know it's not the right thing to do but sometimes I just get overwhelmed with temptation and I do it anyway. One of these situations happened during the period of time that I was doing my Step Ten daily journal. I had an unexpected delay in my travel due to weather and I ended up spending the night in a hotel instead of flying home like I had planned. You guessed it, I ordered a pay-per-view porno movie from the privacy of my hotel room and I viewed it for about 20 minutes while entertaining myself, if you know what I mean. Of course I felt bad about it. I knew it wasn't right. But I don't believe in beating myself up so I just wrote it down in my journal and then I tried to put it behind me.

I got up bright and early the next morning to catch my flight home. When I got home that afternoon I was happy to see my wife, but I was also tired and felt somewhat uncomfortable being with her. My daughter, who was 13 at the time, got home later that evening and immediately she came running up to me to give me a hug and a kiss. I felt uncomfortable about seeing her, too. My daughter seemed to be more aware of the discomfort between us than I was. She said to me, "Daddy, why don't you want to be with me? Is there something wrong with me?" This shocked me, but I quickly regained my wits and I assured her that everything was okay. She didn't question me but I could tell that she didn't believe me either. She went off to her room and I made note of this exchange in my journal. Late that evening, as my wife and I were preparing to go to bed, she said, "Gary, what's wrong? You seem distant like you used to be." I assured her that everything was good, we crawled into bed and I tried to go to sleep.

Two hours later I was still awake and my mind had started to race. I got up, went into the kitchen and began to make some notes in my inventory journal. Then, clear as day, some of the events of the last couple of days jumped right off the pages of my journal at me. I realized that my careless actions of looking at the porn movie had impacted me much like my workaholism had affected me in the past. In the past I had used my work like a drug addict uses drugs. I worked to escape the challenges of life—especially the challenges of intimacy—and now I realized that I had also used the porn movie in much the same way, and it was affecting me negatively just like my workaholism had done. As these things came clear to me, I was writing them down in my journal. The more I wrote down, the more clear-headed I became about the diabolical subtleties of my addictions. I could see that my attempts to "escape" were triggered by the simplest of things like being too tired, feeling lonely or sorry for myself, or being upset about something that I could not control. I also realized that my escapes, i.e., workaholism and porn, had a terrible effect on the people who I loved the most. My workaholism and porn use had been like an invisible poison that was slowly killing me and my family. Even though my family didn't know about the porn movie, its negative impact on me created a negative impact on them. It kept us from having a close relationship with one another. Finally, I realized that the opportunities God was giving me to recover would never exist if I lived indiscriminately. There is too much at stake for me not to dig deep and identify the weak points in my character and my life. Not only too much at stake for me but also too much at stake for my family.

My wife is a very early riser and so early the next morning—it was a Saturday—I sat down with her before the kids got up. I apologized to her for being distant. I acknowledged that I did feel very self-conscious when she tried to be close to me the day before. I told her that I had looked at a porn movie at the hotel and I explained to her what I had learned through my journaling. Amazingly, she didn't shoot me. Now, she wasn't happy at all about me looking at porn, but I think she was very relieved to hear me acknowledge how I get diverted and distracted by things. Interestingly and much to my surprise, she seemed to recognize that I had made a breakthrough in my growth; I'd had an experience that would make my heart more accessible to her.

Later that day I spoke to my daughter. I apologized to her for being distant. I acknowledged that she deserved better from me and I told her of my desire to interact with her in a more relaxed, honest and faithful way. I told her that she was my greatest delight and that I was aware how my past actions had not always conveyed my true love for her. I told her of my commitment to do a better job of being her Dad. I didn't tell her about my use of porn because, as my wife and I had discussed, I knew it would hurt her; she was just too young and she didn't need to know. I may tell her more about my struggles when she is older, but I'll wait until then to decide.

Looking back, I don't think things would have turned out this way had I not been continuously taking my inventory. The things I notice about myself now are different than when I first began the Twelve Steps, but they are no less important for me to deal with. My relationships with my wife and children are much better now. I never dreamed we would laugh so much. My wife will occasionally point out that I am being distant or aloof but I really don't mind her telling me this anymore. It doesn't feel like nagging the way it used to. My kids and I are now better at expressing ourselves to one another. I think they feel better with me and with each other because I am better able to express my love and delight in them.

I am thankful for my sponsor and my counselor who have helped guide me in this experience. Even more, I thank God for being there for me and I thank my family for not giving up on me. I still keep a journal because I am still working Step Ten.

The Everydayness of Progress

"We justify our actions by appearances; God examines our motives."
Proverbs 21:2 *The Message*

"What helps at this point is to see your consequences as your teachers.
You have been sent a lesson to learn. If you don't learn the lesson this
time, it will manifest itself again, and probably in a more painful form
the next time."
- Patrick Carnes, Ph. D.

*We continued to take personal inventory
and when we were wrong, promptly admitted it.*

We need to practice our recovery principles every day. The daily
monitoring of our motives helps us to have an honest view of ourselves,
and this helps to insure that we continue to recover from our addictions.
God doesn't tell us to bring our failures to Him just once. He tells us to
bring our failures to Him continuously, day in and day out. For you see,
recovery is a continuous process of character development. We can't be
what we're not, but with practice we can make progress and move closer
to the ideal example that God gave us in Christ. This means that we need
to have a well-balanced understanding of our real needs and our most
honest feelings. We also need to be ruthlessly honest about the health of
our relationships, and the way that we live our lives when no one is
watching. The degree to which we have been guilty of playing to the
crowd will be the degree to which we place ourselves in jeopardy,
risking a relapse of addictive destruction. We have to be real, everyday.
We have to quit pretending.

When we lack character, we need to admit it to ourselves. We need to
admit it to God and we need to admit it to someone else, too. When we
lack integrity, we need to admit that as well. As we admit our lack of
character and integrity, we open ourselves up to an infusion of God's

transforming grace, which is the most fundamental building block of character and integrity. This kind of construction is very personal. It is more intimate than anything we can ever do on our own, even with or without the help of other people. It is a gift from God and not something that we have earned on our own. The work we do is essential for our growth and recovery and we certainly need help from others, but in the end it is God who changes the condition of the human heart and mind.

As we continue to admit our wrongdoing and as we continue to correct our mistakes whenever and however we can—the best we can—we continue to live within the framework of God's character. God's character continues to be built into us, and His character will help us to think and live more effectively in the future.

Complacency and Overconfidence

"I don't mean to say that I have already achieved these things or that I have already reached perfection! But I keep working toward that day when I will finally be all that Christ Jesus saved me for and wants me to be. No, dear brothers and sisters, I am still not all I should be, but I am focusing all my energies on this one thing. Forgetting the past and looking forward to what lies ahead, I strain to reach the end of the race and receive the prize for which God, through Christ Jesus, is calling us up to heaven."

> Philippians 3:12-14 *NLT*

"As an insurance against 'big-shot-ism,' we can often check ourselves by remembering that we are sober today only by the grace of God and that any success we may be having is far more His success than ours."

> - Alcoholics Anonymous

We continued to take personal inventory and when we were wrong, promptly admitted it.

We do our recovery work everyday because our addictions threaten us everyday. They never take a day off. Looking back, we'll see that we've never really known when or how our addictions might strike. How many times have we found ourselves suffering a bout of addictive self-destruction, and at the same time asking ourselves *How did this happen again? What did I do wrong this time?* Usually, the answer to this question was not that we did something wrong, but it was because we were not doing the simple but essential things that keep us from the slippery slopes of relapse.

Complacency and overconfidence are probably the most common reasons why people relapse. This is why we need to guard ourselves against pride, arrogance and overconfidence. We need to stay in close honest contact with our sponsors, our counselors and our recovery partners in order to keep our heads clear and free from the complacency and overconfidence that is so dangerous to us. As we humbly accept and admit our failures, our failures will increase our motivation for change and growth. As we maintain the habit of continuously sharing the good, the bad and the ugly parts of our lives, we will continue to become the men and the women that we have always wanted to be.

On our bad days, we tend to think about our failures. On our good days, we tend to think about our successes. But, on our best days, we tend not to think about ourselves at all, because we are too busy thinking about God and other people.

What God Gives

"One day one of the local officials asked him, 'Good Teacher, what must I do to deserve eternal life?' Jesus said, 'Why are you calling me good? No one is good—only God. You know the commandments, don't you? No illicit sex, no killing, no stealing, no lying, honor your father and mother.' He said, 'I've kept them all for as long as I can remember.' When Jesus heard that, he said, 'Then there's only one thing left to do: Sell everything you own and give it away to the poor. You will have riches in heaven. Then come, follow me.' This was the last thing the official expected to hear. He was very rich and became terribly sad. He was holding on tight to a lot of things and not about to let them go. Seeing his reaction, Jesus said, 'Do you have any idea how difficult it is for people who have it all to enter God's kingdom? I'd say it's easier to thread a camel through a needle's eye than get a rich person into God's kingdom.' 'Then who has any chance at all?' the others asked. 'No chance at all,' Jesus said, 'if you think you can pull it off by yourself. Every chance in the world if you trust God to do it.'"

Luke 18:18-28 *The Message*

"Grace fills empty spaces, but it can only enter where there is a void to receive it, and it is grace itself which makes this void."
- Simone Weil

We continued to take personal inventory and when we were wrong, promptly admitted it.

Luke 18 tells the story of a successful man, and it shows us why he is a good example of how we can hinder our own growth. The man in the story enthusiastically came to Jesus seeking to increase his quality of life, but he walked away devastated with sadness and sorrow. Apparently, this man's life included wealth, talent, social standing and religious excellence. But this wasn't enough for him. He wanted more. Can you relate?

This man had confused personal success—and having the good things in life—with a satisfying life. Knowing this, and knowing that having a good life alone will never satisfy anyone, Jesus did not give the man what he wanted. Instead, Jesus challenged the man's virtue by questioning his lustful desire for more material, social and religious goodness, which the man called "eternal life." Scripture tells us how the man had no effective response to Jesus' challenge because he wanted what *he* wanted, more than what Jesus had to give. Let no one be confused here. The man had all the information that he needed to know. He had every opportunity to make the right choice. He was fully responsible for making the decision for his life, and he was fully responsible for his own sadness. This is because his sadness was not a result of Jesus' challenge; it was the result of his own inability to let go of the things he valued so much. It was not *things* that were his problem; it was his *attachment* to things that kept him stuck where he was. The man's problem would have been easily solved if he had just been willing to let go and follow Jesus.

How many times have we been in a similar situation? How many times have we sensed that God wanted us to fess up and admit that we were holding on to well-polished idols? Perhaps God is pointing out certain things like personal qualities, talents, desires, interests, reliances or relationships that show that we are not as close to God as we would like others to believe. The message for all of us is clear. Jesus is calling us to let go of the things that we think we need or things we think we are entitled to. But, it's more than that. The calling Jesus makes is not really about things at all; it is about letting go. It is about our priorities, our relationships with things and our willingness to let go of things so that we can be free to be filled with the better things that God has for us.

"Sell all that you have and follow me." – Jesus

A Deeper Point of View

"Living then, as every one of you does, in pure grace, it's important that you not misinterpret yourselves as people who are bringing this goodness to God. No, God brings it all to you. The only accurate way to understand ourselves is by what God is and by what he does for us, not by what we are and what we do for him."

> Romans 12:3 *The Message*

"God asks no man whether he will accept life. This is not the choice. You must take it. The only question is how."

> - Henry Ward Beecher

We continued to take personal inventory and when we were wrong, promptly admitted it.

Being sober from our addictions is a wonderful thing. It is what we wanted when we first started this recovery journey of ours. But, as God leads us through all the puddles, lakes, and oceans of life, He will invariably lead us into new and uncharted waters. Shallow waters are for children. Let us continue to grow, let us reach out and swim for the deep waters.

- What do we think when we think about ourselves?
- What are the things that we value the most?
- How is our identity shaped by the things we value?
- Do our possessions and priorities keep us from experiencing God's deeper fellowship?
- Do our relationships keep us from relating to God at the most intimate level?
- What personal qualities do we have that we know we should change?
- How do we rely on our talents to make us acceptable to people and to God?
- What do we want that conflicts with God's ideal for our lives?

- Are there interests in our lives that are questionable or inappropriate?
- Do we use our ministry, or our service to others, as a way of expressing our goodness?
- Why do we feel the need to prove our goodness?
- Are we more devoted to what we think we should be than to what God is making us into?

Questions like these help us to look beyond our addictions and gain a deeper view into our internal character. The more we are willing to let go and change, the more we will experience God's power changing us on the inside. As we are willing to let go of our subtle idolatries, our perceptions about them will change and our interest in them will disappear. We will discover that the discouragement and the disillusionment that we feel from time to time are not really bad things. They can actually be good for us because they reveal how we have loved ourselves and our lives—or even our own devotion to Jesus—more than we have loved Jesus himself.

God's promise of new life is a promise of himself and the Life that He is. The only eternal promise that He makes is that we will have Him forever. In the end only He will remain. Everything else will pass away. As we learn to be content with Jesus and Jesus alone, we will receive increasing joy amidst the discouragement and sadness that comes our way.

Step Eleven

Sought through prayer and meditation to improve our conscious contact with God as we understood Him, praying only for the knowledge of His will for us and the power to carry that out.

As human beings we are inclined to seek out and search for the things that we need and want. We do it instinctively in almost every area of our lives. We search for the best bargains at the mall, we look for the best food for our families, and we research information related to politics, healthcare, investments, and education. Seeking and searching seems to be in our DNA. Even our addictions show how we have looked high and low, seeking relief from our pain and the nagging sense of futility that we have felt. Above everything else, and often without realizing it, we have been searching for a meaningful connection that will satisfy us at the most intimate and personal spiritual level.

Step Eleven is a practice that helps us focus our efforts and make good use of our instinct to search. It helps us learn more about God, to be closer to God and to have our hearts, our minds and our lives molded by God in deep, intimate, pragmatic ways. Step Eleven is not a religious activity. It's more like our morning coffee, an evening conversation or an intimate encounter with our loved one. It is intimate and personal and eternal. Step Eleven brings spontaneity into our relationship with God. This is because our relationship with God, just like all other relationships, requires that we actively engage the one we want to be close to. As we begin to relate with God in these ways, we will learn to enjoy Him immensely and we'll want to be with Him often and always.

A Different Desire

"Let petitions and praises shape your worries into prayers, letting God know your concerns. Before you know it, a sense of God's wholeness, everything coming together for good, will come and settle down. It's wonderful what happens when Christ displaces worry at the center of your life."

>   Philippians 4:6-7 *The Message*

"We must be motivated from within, not from without. We must live our lives before God, knowing that He sees all and that our reward will come from Him if we persist in doing what He has asked us to do."

>   - Joyce Meyer

Sought through prayer and meditation to improve our conscious contact with God as we understood Him, praying only for the knowledge of His will for us and the power to carry that out.

We have failed to meet our own needs. Everything we've tried to make ourselves right has ended in failure. Surrendering our lives to God is more of an act of desperation than of virtue. We didn't surrender because we were good or honorable or because we thought we had our lives under control. We surrendered our lives to Him in order to save our lives!

We must never lose sight of the fact that God is never gained by virtue. He is only discovered when a bankrupt man or woman seeks Him. Desperate, every one of us has had our own personal reasons why we surrendered our lives to God. Some reasons seemed like really good ones and others seemed very selfish, and that's okay because any and every reason to seek God and recover from our brokenness is a good one. And there is never a bad reason to ask God for help.

In recovery, we learn to seek God for better and more important reasons than the reasons we had when we first started. As we progress, we learn to seek Him and to surrender to Him for the best reason: God himself. We came to God because we had to, but we stay with God because we learn to live in His grace. There is no other place for us to find a life that is worth living.

Darnell's Story

I have never had a better life than the one I have today. For the first time I have the life I'd hoped for when I was a kid. Growing up, I saw how my friends enjoyed life. They had a positive outlook that always escaped me. My days were spent in self-loathing and envy and these feelings drove me to desperate measures. I was always trying to escape the way I felt but I never could.

But, thankfully things have changed. I got the help I needed with my drug addiction and I made the decision to give my life to God. As a result, today I am thankful to be alive. I am learning to be content with the way things are and I have hope for the future. Now I must say that even with as good as I am doing, I still feel a restlessness within me. I still want something more. It's like I've been on a very long journey to get home and while seeing my home in the distance, the last mile is all uphill.

My deep yearnings have not disappeared, but now that God has met me in my pain, the way I interpret my feelings has changed. My feelings are not the chronic emptiness they once were. It's hard for me to explain. My painful feelings are more like the kind of soreness that comes from good exercise. I feel a longing, like the longing for a loved one that I know is coming home to be with me soon.

Having come to know the greatest joy in the universe—God—I have been enlarged so that I am ready for more of whatever good God has to give me. My appetite for badness—my addiction that is—has lessened and my appetite for goodness has increased. My soul is not yet completely satisfied, but it is filled up with a joy that overrides my yearning when I direct myself to God whom I know through Christ Jesus.

I see life simpler now. It's as simple as this: with God there is life; without God there is no life. This simple principle transforms everything I think, feel and do. With it, I become the kind of man who lives privately just like I would if everyone were watching me. I wrote this poem as a prayer. It sums it up for me.

Dear God,
The more I seek You, the more I find You; The more I find You, the more I love You; The more I love You, the more I seek You.

Soul Yearnings

"Show me the path where I should walk, O Lord; point out the right road for me to follow. Lead me by your truth and teach me, for you are the God who saves me. All day long I put my hope in you."
Psalm 25:4-5 *NLT*

"In prayer, real prayer, we begin to think God's thoughts after Him: to desire the things he desires, to love the things he loves, to will the things he wills. Progressively, we are taught to see things from his point of view."
- Richard J. Foster

Sought through prayer and meditation to improve our conscious contact with God as we understood Him, praying only for the knowledge of His will for us and the power to carry that out.

Our sponsors, our mentors, spiritual directors and our counselors have helped us and will continue to help us grow in our recovery. While they help us, they are not the resource or the power that gives us growth. That is done by God's Holy Spirit. As our *"new man in Christ"* grows within us, we will develop a personality and identity that is much more suited to what God created us to be than anything we could have hoped ourselves to be. This new identity is much more from the influence of God working deep within us than it is from what we have learned or observed from others. The examples that others have given us are very good, but we are called to something more personal and more unique to who we are as individuals. We must not confuse a teacher with *The Teacher*. Human teachers come and go, but God will never leave us and He will not forsake His commitment to work His best into every area of our lives.

Our joy in recovery will suffer if we don't exhibit the humble diligence that leads to intimacy with God. The bigger our ego gets, the smaller

God gets, and as God's presence in our life grows, our ego will shrink correspondingly. Only after—and never without the intentional application of hard disciplined work—will we grow up. Growth will not remove our human imperfections, but it will enlarge us spiritually, molding us to be more like God intended us to be. We are responsible to be diligent in our pursuit of what God wants us to be. We are responsible for living out the miraculous purpose for which He created us.

One of the great things that will come out of our walk with God will be the stories that come from our life experience. When we share them, our life experiences will encourage others much like we have been encouraged by those who've shared theirs with us. For you see, God takes all the broken pieces of our lives and He creates something worthwhile for everyone. While the details of our stories will be different from one another, the fundamentals will be the same. In recovery, we all admit how our failures and our addictions proved how alone we had been. We accepted our need for God and then His love broke through to us. He reached into our aloneness and we reached back for Him. We had been like adulterous lovers, awkward and embarrassed, sneaking in the back door, not knowing what to say. But God made the first move to listen to us and get close to us and now, because we want to get close to Him too, we make the second move which is to pray. Prayer takes us out of our aloneness.

Prayer Makes Us Real

"Keep on asking, and you will be given what you ask for. Keep on looking and you will find. Keep on knocking and the door will be opened. For everyone who asks, receives. Everyone who seeks, finds. And the door is opened to everyone who knocks."

> Matthew 7:7-8 *NLT*

"Instead of all these, the answer that he gives, I think, is himself. If we go to him for anything else, he may send us away empty or he may not. But if we go to him for himself, I believe that we go away always with this deepest of all our hungers filled."

> - Frederick Buechner

Sought through prayer and meditation to improve our conscious contact with God as we understood Him, praying only for the knowledge of His will for us and the power to carry that out.

Everyone prays. We all pray in one way or another, often without realizing it. Instinctively, we have the need to connect with permanence, and prayer can be considered as our personal attempt to reach and touch eternity. Prayer helps us make sense of our lives. It helps us sort through tragedy and heartbreak and locate the treasures that are hidden inside of misfortune.

Many of us have been trained to think of prayer as a religious activity or duty. Somewhere along the way we were sold a bill of goods. Someone convinced us that prayer had to be done in a certain way that was scripted or traditional according to certain previously defined standards. This is not true. Prayer is never limited in any way because God is not limited in any way. Prayer may be well-planned or it may be spontaneous. It may be formal or it may be casual and conversational. It may be traditional and religious or it may be radical. Prayer can be expressed in many different ways, and it is always real and effective as long as we are real and sincere with it. Prayer is not a matter of technique. It is a matter of attitude and openness.

The impact of prayer is reduced if we think of it as a demand or a duty that is required of us. We objectify prayer, we objectify God and we objectify ourselves if prayer is ever reduced to anything less than an act of intimacy. When reduced, prayer becomes nothing more important than washing dishes or making beds. And while these are obviously very good and very necessary things, they are not the things that help us, heal us or bring us into closeness with God. Prayer is more of an opportunity. It is a calling. It is a picking up of the ringing phone and completing the connection that God has made available to us through Christ. Prayer is the way we engage God at a personal intimate level. And while we are engaging God through prayer, we are engaging ourselves at a personal and intimate level, too.

Prayer is a dialogue. It puts us at the kitchen table with coffee mug in hand, ready to enjoy a special closeness with our loved one. It is cognitive and intuitive. It's a spiritual openness that increases our oneness with God and with ourselves. Prayer ushers us into private communion with the perfect Father— God. And while He is perfect, our prayers don't need to be perfect. The only thing prayer needs to be is real. What we don't know how to say, God's Spirit will say for us. He understands everything, even the things we do not know or cannot express. Prayer, in essence, breaks the silence. It closes the distance between God and us. It heals our splintered hearts and our broken minds. It helps us to know what we feel and it helps us to think better. Prayer fulfills our need to be known. Prayer teaches us to accept God's unconditional approval, and it teaches us to accept ourselves at the same time. Prayer teaches us to recognize treasures that we have not noticed before. We will be able to make sense of difficulties and hardships. Praying privately helps us to be more honest and more true to ourselves.

It opens us up. It is the sound we make—the spiritual sound—when we don't know what to say or how to say it.

Prayer catapults us into the frontier of an authentic spiritual life.

Prayer Changes Us

"And yet the reason you don't have what you want is that you don't ask God for it. And even when you do ask, you don't get it because your motive is wrong – you want only what will give you pleasure."
    James 4:3 *NLT*

"Drawing near to God is, in fact, the beginning of union!"
    - Jeanne Guyon

Sought through prayer and meditation to improve our conscious contact with God as we understood Him, praying only for the knowledge of His will for us and the power to carry that out.

Prayer is the most relevant thing we do. If we are to be free from our addictions, free from our compulsions and free from self-tyranny, we will have to become people who pray consistently, without stopping. Prayer must become part of us much like eating or breathing, bathing and sleeping. The kind of prayer we need is a personal, open and ongoing interaction with God—the type of interaction that brings insight and understanding, helping us to resolve the catastrophes of our past and increase our hopefulness for the future. Ongoing prayer helps us know exactly who we are and what we should do at any moment in time. It builds integrity in us, making us well-balanced and whole. Prayer keeps us alert and ready to live well during any difficulty that may come our way.

Prayer helps us to work with God to build our future. It plays a huge role in determining what kind of people we will be and what kind of impact we will have on the world. It may be helpful to pray for others to change, but it is always more important to pray that we will change. Prayer changes us and—as we are changed—the influence we have on our surroundings will change, too. Prayer gives us new perspectives. It changes our priorities. Instead of praying for things we want or for things we need, we should pray that we will be increasingly motivated to bring ourselves closer to God.

If we pray for anything less than God himself, we may go away disappointed, having learned just how idolatrous we still are. But when we pray seeking a closer walk with Him, we will always find our deepest longings fulfilled, often before we know what our deepest longings really are.

Be Still, Be Quiet, Listen

"Anyone who drinks the water I give will never thirst—not ever. The water I give will be an artesian spring within, gushing fountains of endless life."

> John 4:14 *The Message*

"Let therefore our chiefest endeavor be, to meditate upon the life of Christ."

> - Thomas à Kempis

Sought through prayer and meditation to improve our conscious contact with God as we understood Him, praying only for the knowledge of His will for us and the power to carry that out.

Relationships are a two-way street. We need to share what we think and feel with others *and* we need to be good listeners, too, if we want successful relationships with those we care about. Our relationship with God is no different. He listens to what we say, and we need to listen for what He has to say to us.

Meditation is a practice that is committed to hearing God's voice and understanding the directions He gives us. We have worked very hard in our recovery, but meditation will be different from the work we have done so far. This is because meditation is not about *doing* anything; it is about quietness of mind, relaxation of body and openness of heart.

Meditation is the flip side of prayer. It completes the dialogue that takes place between God and us. We speak when we pray, but we listen when we meditate. In fact, prayer without listening to God is probably not healthy for us. Our prayers become very self-centered if we don't listen to what God has to say. Very often the best thing we can do for our spiritual growth is to stop. Stop working. Stop playing. Stop everything.

Be still. Be quiet. *Listen.* We should set all our distractions aside so we can make time and space in our minds and our hearts for God alone, so we can listen for how He comes close to us in the time and space we create for Him. As we do this, He will reorganize our wants and our worries in ways that are healthier for us and more useful for His purposes. God speaks to us not because of our special abilities, but because we are listening, wanting to hear what He has to say to us. Actually, He is always speaking to us. But only when we listen will our ears tune into what He is saying.

Learning to listen to God is simple but, just like learning other things, it takes some practice. We learn to meditate by meditating. We start, get distracted, start again, get distracted and then start again. With time, we learn to become more capable of hearing and discerning the voice of God. This is not effort like most of us think about effort, because it takes nothing from us. We just open ourselves up like we would open our hand to accept a gift. It's like going outside when it's raining if we want to get wet. It is the simplest of all things we do. It's like enjoying music, which requires no physical effort on our part. Listening requires only the intention and desire to accept the sound that someone else makes. It's natural, like a mother's intuitive ear that is tuned to the slightest sound her sleeping child makes. Meditation—listening for the sound of God—is a filling of our heart and mind with God's heart and mind. It gives us a deepening friendship with Jesus, because Jesus appreciates us listening to Him like any friend of ours would appreciate it when we listen to them. And as we listen— meditate, that is—we can expect God to speak to us at the spiritual level.

Our imaginations will run freely as we meditate, like a child's does. This is a good thing, because God gives us imagination for a purpose and, while our addictions deaden our capacity for creative thinking, meditation enlarges our capacity for creativity. Listening for God opens us up to the wonderful world of possibilities and goal setting. We will believe all sorts of wonderful ways that God will reveal himself to us, change us, restore us and use us. But there is one thing we must never lose sight of. God has no obligation to serve us. He has committed himself to love and care for us eternally, but He is not obligated in anyway to give us everything we think we should have. We must not allow meditation to become a breeding ground for selfishness and self-centeredness, which are most dangerous when they take on a religious tone. Guard against self-deception. If we are serious about walking with God, we will prefer obedience over comfort and blessing.

The discipline of meditation helps to balance our minds and our emotions, and the best way to make the most of our commitment to this discipline is to meditate on Scripture. God gives us His Word to help us build a well-balanced point of view. The Bible is the most obvious and consistent way that He speaks to us. It is the grounding rod of everything we do in our walk with God. Making Scripture a daily part of our lives keeps our disciplines of prayer and meditation centered on God and His will for our lives. Without a consistent dose of Scripture, we will never have a strong walk with God. And no matter how much we study the Bible, our disciplines will be ineffective if we do not have the foundation of deep personal humility, which comes from brokenness. Humility helps give us a balanced view of God's Word. And we have to have a balanced understanding of Scripture in order to have a balanced perspective about our lives.

The purpose of Scripture is to reveal God to us, not to give us knowledge. Just learning facts about God and Christian history really doesn't do us a whole lot of good. This doesn't mean that facts aren't important because they are. They give us reference and context to help us better understand the compassion that God has for all people. Our goal in studying the Bible makes all the difference. Do we want to increase our knowledge *about* God, or do we want to increase our closeness *with* God? This is the profound question that is always before us.

For you see, the Bible is more than just a history book. It contains the breath and life of God. Our commitment to meditate on Scripture opens us up to inhale the breath of God. This will transform us. The love, the friendship, the instruction, and the eternal message of compassion that are in Scripture will move off the pages of the Bible and into us. We should think of Scripture in the same way that a man who's dying of thirst would think about water. We should want it like someone who is starving would want a pizza. We want to drink it, eat it, consume it. We want to get Scripture into us so that it can nourish us, strengthen us and make us healthy and strong. Taking God's Word into us will teach us to listen intently, to speak softly, and to live powerfully.

Priority

"Trust God from the bottom of your heart; don't try to figure out everything on your own. Listen for God's voice in everything you do, everywhere you go; he's the one who will keep you on track."

Proverbs 3:5-6 *The Message*

"We take our efforts seriously, while knowing that serious results are from God. We remain intent and dogged in pursuit of our disciplines, in the working of the steps, but dismiss at all times the notion that our work is enough. It never is. Our miracles come from God, and He offers them in conjunction with our work."

\- Oswald Chambers

Sought through prayer and meditation to improve our conscious contact with God as we understood Him, praying only for the knowledge of His will for us and the power to carry that out.

Self-centeredness is cunning, it is baffling and it is powerful. We slip into it often without knowing it. And nothing will kill our recovery faster than when self-centeredness lies hidden in our religious activity. Our commitments to pray and meditate will not make us immune. We will trip up sometimes because we lose sight of the fact that we are not the one who brings good gifts to us. Good gifts come from God alone. We must remember that our best intentions and efforts got us addicted. So, we must never rely on our efforts alone, no matter how good or well-intentioned they are. It is God who makes the difference in our lives. Yes, we are responsible for being disciplined and intentional in our responsibilities, because we will not grow spiritually if we do not apply ourselves. But discipline and hard work are never enough to overcome our addictions or conquer the self-centeredness that lurks within us.

All of the growth we've had so far has come from God, and the growth we experience in the future will come from Him, too. Carving this simple principle onto our hearts and minds will keep us motivated to keep up with our spiritual disciplines. It will keep us moving along the path of God's spiritual care.

The Point of Our Prayer

"Are you seeking great things for yourself Don't do it! But don't be discouraged!"
>Jeremiah 45:5 *NLT*

"In this life we cannot always do great things. But we can do small things with great love."
>- Mother Teresa

Sought through prayer and meditation to improve our conscious contact with God as we understood Him, praying only for the knowledge of His will for us and the power to carry that out.

The following prayers are examples of how others have expressed themselves to God. They are a template we can use to express ourselves, and to remind ourselves that our relationship with God is always the most important thing. We don't own ourselves anymore. We belong to God. And He can do with us whatever He knows to be best. As we meditate on the following prayers; the people who wrote them will become like friends to us. Their prayers will help us move and grow toward God.

The Serenity Prayer by theologian Reinhold Niebuhr
God grant me the serenity to accept the things I cannot change; courage
to change the things I can; and the wisdom to know the difference.
Living one day at a time; accepting hardship as a pathway to peace;
taking, as Jesus did, this sinful world as it is, not as I would have it:
trusting that You will make all things right if I surrender to Your will;
that I may be reasonably happy in this life and supremely happy with
You forever in the next. Amen

Prayer of Saint Francis of Assisi

Lord, make me an instrument of your peace. Where there is hatred, let me sow love; where there is injury, pardon; where there is doubt, faith; where there is despair, hope; where there is darkness, light; and where there is sadness, joy. Lord, grant that I may not so much seek to be consoled as to console; to be understood as to understand; to be loved as to love. For it is in giving that we receive; it is in pardoning that we are pardoned; and it is in dying that we are born to eternal life. Amen

Operation Integrity Prayer

Dear God, I pray that I will learn to desire obedience more than blessing or comfort and to know that the greatest blessing in life is to live obedient to Your will. May I learn to better give up my will and find my complete and total satisfaction in Your will. My self-centeredness destroys me, but seeking You and doing Your will brings life to me. Realizing this, I have decided that my mind, my heart and my will, will be directed to You. I will find my purpose and identity in knowing You more personally and living more powerfully according to your Spirit.
Amen

Step Three Prayer from Alcoholics Anonymous

God, I offer myself to Thee—to build with me and to do with me as Thou wilt. Relieve me of the bondage of self, that I may better do Thy will. Take away my difficulties, that victory over them may bear witness to those I would help of Thy Power, Thy love, and Thy way of life. May I do Thy will always! Amen

Step Seven Prayer from Alcoholics Anonymous

My Creator, I am now willing that You should have all of me, good and bad. I pray that You now remove from me every single defect of character which stands in the way of my usefulness to You and my fellows. Grant me strength, as I go out from here, to do Your bidding.
Amen

Step Twelve

Having had a spiritual awakening as the result of these Steps, we tried to carry the message to others, and to practice these principles in all our affairs.

We first began our recovery journey because we needed to heal an addiction. And, while we have begun to heal from our addiction, other things that we might not have expected have begun to happen as well. We are developing healthier and more honest perspectives. Our relationships are improving. And, best of all, we continue to receive the ongoing gift of spiritual transformation.

The transformation that God gives is limitless in how it affects those of us who seek Him. This is because of the countless ways that God positively affects our lives. He changes and improves us in every way. For instance, we used to hide in shame, but now we feel blessed when other people want to get to know us. We have come to realize there is no reason for us to hide ourselves away anymore. We want to walk in the light, enjoying healthier points of view. We are now able to see how our addictions are like deadly storms in the ocean; they motivate us to seek the safe harbor of God. And as we set our moorings deep into God, He transforms us into powerful lovers of people. This is the fundamental essence of the spiritual awakening that is happening in us. Nothing will hold us back when we walk with God. We have every good reason to share *all* of our life experiences with others.

Our responsibility going forward is no different than it was when we first began our journey. Our job is to continue to apply Twelve Step recovery principles to our lives, to walk with God, and to help others do the same.

Destiny Arrives and We Show Up

"Summing it all up, friends, I'd say you'll do best by filling your minds and meditating on things true, noble, reputable, authentic, compelling, gracious - the best, not the worst; the beautiful, not the ugly; things to praise, not things to curse. Put into practice what you learned from me, what you heard and saw and realized. Do that, and God, who makes everything work together, will work you into his most excellent harmonies."

Philippians 4:8-9 *The Message*

"Listen to your life. See it for the fathomless mystery that it is. In the boredom and pain of it no less than in the excitement and gladness: touch, taste, smell your way to the holy and hidden heart of it because in the last analysis all moments are key moments, and life itself is grace."

- Frederick Buechner

Having had a spiritual awakening as the result of these Steps, we tried to carry the message to others, and to practice these principles in all our affairs.

None of us ever meant to get addicted to anything. We didn't ask for it, and we didn't intend it. In the beginning, addiction was the last thing we ever thought would happen to us. But, nonetheless, we got addicted anyway. In the end, no matter how naive or innocent we might have been, we have had to confess that our addictions have been deeply rooted in our bad thinking and our lack of a real faith in God. We now know how a lack of authentic faith and bad thinking go hand in hand.

Recovery became possible for us when we admitted our need and began to accept the help that God made available. Making this confession helped us hope for a better life than the one we had known in the past. We began to see that God had bigger and better plans for us than we did. Following His plan, both our addictions and our healing became a pathway. They became like stepping-stones to a revolutionary kind of personal transformation that we never could have envisioned when we first started our journey. And along the way, we receive much more than we ever could have expected or anticipated. We have been changed on the inside. We have learned things that no book could ever teach us. We have gained insights and had experiences that we could never get in any classroom or from any other person, either. There is a new presence and reality within us and it is more than our senses can identify, more than our physical bodies can contain and very, very much more than we can ever explain. We have God's Spirit working inside of us and through us.

The way we experience recovery is a unique and personalized gift from God. We receive it and experience it on an individual and personal basis. It is a redemption that is deeply intimate between God and us, together, just the two of us, connecting and being close. This is why none of us will ever have the exact same experience in recovery or with God. And while we all have our own intimate encounter with God, the recovery experience He gives is not ours to keep for ourselves. We must be willing to share it if we want to keep it long-term. And as we share our experience with others, we will discover that we have much more in common than we ever realized before. This is how God expands and multiplies the intimate life He has shared with us.

A New Purpose for Our Lives

"But Jesus said, 'No, go home to your friends, and tell them what wonderful things the Lord has done for you and how merciful he has been.'"

Mark 5:19 *NLT*

"If you will agree with God's purpose, He will bring not only your conscious level but also all the deeper levels of your life, which you yourself cannot reach, into perfect harmony."

- Oswald Chambers

Having had a spiritual awakening as the result of these Steps, we tried to carry the message to others, and to practice these principles in all our affairs

Pain and fear are often two of our greatest motivators. Pain grabs our attention, and fear either paralyzes us or it shakes us into doing things that are usually destructive. This is how our impulsive attempts to avoid pain and fear have deepened our addictions. But, thankfully, things have begun to change. Hope and humility give us the willingness to go through pain instead of escaping it, and the ability to address fear instead of running from it.

We become the kind of people who can face fear and endure pain when we see that a more intimate walk with God lies ahead for us. This intimacy with God motivates us to keep moving forward and leave our addictions behind. God teaches us to not fear pain like we used to. He teaches us to handle fear in healthy ways. We learn to benefit from our pain and fear as we accept them as opportunities to exercise our faith in God. The strength of our faith is not the issue at hand, because walking with God is not a matter of how big or how small our faith is. If we have faith in God, in whatever amount, we have enough. Our faith, after all, is in Him, not in ourselves. This faithful thinking moves us to the place where our addictions just won't make sense to us anymore. Our addictions never really helped us, you know; they only distracted us. We don't want that old life anymore. So, why would ever want to go back to them again? We want God's best now, and we are willing to do whatever it takes to have His best, even when it is painful and even when we feel afraid.

In the past, most of us have thought of ourselves as physical beings who were trying to have spiritual experiences, but now we think of ourselves as spiritual beings who are having physical experiences in ways that are uniquely designed for us, individually, by God. We will enjoy some of these experiences and not others. We will laugh sometimes and we will cry sometimes. No matter what the circumstances are, and no matter what emotions and feelings we have, things for us have become wonderfully simple. We are people who have suffered terrible addictions, but now we are people who enjoy God's best today and everyday. We don't judge our lives by our circumstances; we judge them by the freedom of our heart. For you see, through God's grace coupled with our surrender, we become the most blessed of all people. We know this because God only judges us by the standard of His love and righteousness that's been displayed through Christ. We, on the other hand, judge ourselves more harshly. We judge ourselves by our willingness or our unwillingness to respond to His love through our obedience.

Recognizing how blessed we are gives us gratitude for our addictions. A grateful heart helps us to look back and see our addictions as a kind of training ground. They have prepared us to become the kind of men and women who can share God's grace with others in very dynamic ways. More than most, we embody the progressive prodigal experience of hopelessness, selfishness, disaster, desperation, whimpering cries for help, grace given, grace received and life resurrected. By God's design, there is no better plan for us than what we have experienced. Our purpose in life going forward is to seek, discover and experience God as

Jesus Christ knows God, and as we receive the benefits of knowing God, we will encourage others to seek, discover and experience God for themselves.

We are all prodigals in one way or another. And understanding this is at the core of our transformation.

Living Life for Others

"Live creatively, friends. If someone falls into sin, forgivingly restore him, saving your critical comments for yourself. You might be needing forgiveness before the day's out."

Galatians 6:1 *The Message*

"You can't keep it unless you give it away."
- Alcoholics Anonymous

Having had a spiritual awakening as the result of these Steps, we tried to carry the message to others, and to practice these principles in all our affairs.

We have good reasons to be proud of our growth, and we should also be proud of those who are growing alongside of us. Not proud in a boastful or self-confident way, but in a way that acknowledges and appreciates the role we have played in our own recovery. We have, after all, been desperate enough and smart enough to partner with God in the building of our new life. With His power and our willingness, we are ready and well-equipped to give goodness and love to whomever we encounter. This doesn't mean that we have fully recovered from our addictions, because we haven't. We must remember that overconfidence and complacency can set us up, and then we easily become our own greatest downfall. We must never forget how we have been addicted in the past, and we must never think that we cannot be addicted again in the future.

God, in His loving way, will give us our reminders. Every now and then, our brains will make a spontaneous wrong turn and we will once again experience the conflicted impulse and desire of addictive thinking. Every one of us will have our temptations and mental lapses, especially when we are tired or stressed or hurting or afraid. So, let us never forget that we are people who are at risk of relapse. Our challenges start with our thinking, but it is not our first thought that gets us into trouble really. A first wayward thought is nothing more than a temptation, and temptation is nothing but a fork in the road. It is a place where we have to make a choice. The real concern is what choice we will make when we're tempted. What we do with the first thought will make all the difference for us. With our second thought we choose to continue to walk with God and enjoy the life that He gives, or go the way of sin and relapse, suffering the inevitable consequences that come with sin and relapse.

The only way to ensure our ability to make good choices in times of temptation is with our ongoing spiritual submission to God's way of living through faith and obedience. He alone has the power to keep us safe from our selfish nature, but He cannot help us unless we obey Him! Sometimes the temptations will be uncomfortable, and other times they may be miserable. So, let us continue to admit that we are powerless over our addictions and that our lives are unmanageable without God's care and control of our lives. Every time that we feel the urge to go back to our addictions and we don't, the obsessions and compulsions associated with our addictions will lose some of their power. They will never go away completely, but new attachments for goodness are being made inside of us every moment that we walk with God by doing our recovery work. Ultimately, if we persist, these new good attachments will gain strength over the old bad ones. Increasingly, we will lose interest in our own life compared to the expanding thrill of giving God and His life to others. We'll want to share the spiritual revolution that God is giving to us with the whole world.

Possessed by God

"Those of us who are strong and able in the faith need to step in and lend a hand to those who falter, and not just do what is most convenient for us. Strength is for service, not status. Each one of us needs to look after the good of the people around us, asking ourselves, 'How can I help?'"
　　　Romans 15:1 *The Message*

"The great illusion of leadership is to think that man can be led out of the desert by someone who has never been there."
　- Henri Nouwen

Having had a spiritual awakening as the result of these Steps, we tried to carry the message to others, and to practice these principles in all our affairs.

Our new life should be considered a gift, but it is not without cost. It carries with it a responsibility that, if left unmet, proves that we do not really appreciate the opportunity we have been given. Since we have admitted how unmanageable our lives had become, we cannot honestly claim ownership of our lives anymore. Our addictions have owned us in the past, but in recovery our lives are given over to God. Our worthless and tattered lives have been bought through the death of God's Son, Jesus. And, the opportunity we have for a new life has been assured through His resurrection. This is, in a nutshell, the very basis of our faith. And this is why God is free to care for us in whatever way He thinks is best.

As we become assured of God's active redemption, we will increasingly receive the most life-changing of all good gifts—the gift of gratitude. Gratitude nourishes all of our God-given desires. It makes every area of our life an act of worship and praise. Even our shortcomings give glory to God when we are grateful for them. With gratitude, we return to God a portion of the goodness that He continually gives to us. For we need to always remember that the gifts He gives are not ours to own. They are not to be used for our benefit and prosperity. The gifts that God gives to us are only ours to hold, to appreciate and to pass along to others.

What started with Bill Wilson and Dr. Bob Smith—two alcoholics helping each other—has resulted in a movement that today helps millions of people recover from alcoholism and drug addiction. Alcoholics Anonymous has also spawned the Al-Anon movement, which helps millions of co-dependents and families of alcoholics worldwide. Additionally, AA has inspired the development of numerous other Twelve Step programs that help countless numbers of people recover from many different forms of addiction. Just like Bill Wilson and Dr. Smith, our lives can be multiplied many, many times over when we are willing to share them with others. Once again, this is because God's power is without limit. If we are willing to do our recovery work faithfully, we will become a gift to the whole world one moment, one situation, one person at a time.

The greatest needs of our day will not be met by counselors, by doctors or by experts, politicians or professionals. The greatest needs of our day will be met by recovering people like us. We are grateful leaders in pain suffered, and humble leaders in recovery gained. We are men and women who, having fought the fight for our own lives, now, more importantly, are willing to join the fight for the lives of others. The greatest need in our world today remains the same as it has always been: godly men and women who display a quality of character and life that ignites in others a desire to know God in a way that changes them.

And, on top of it all, each of us has a special role to play. God has given each of us, individually, a message to share and a story to tell. Yes, we are called to tell our story. We are called to tell how we had been blind and desperate and lost in our addictions. And we are called to tell about how God answered us when we, having gotten to our wits end, humbly asked Him for help.

Everyone needs to know that their secrets, struggles, problems, addictions and sins do not need to keep them from God. They need to hear that Jesus has solved all of these problems as far as God is concerned. Our job is to simply share the basic facts of our life and how God has given us our recovery experience. We don't have to go into great detail or feel any pressure to perform, either. God is responsible for the results, not us. And, the people with whom we share are responsible for what they do with whatever we share with them. We just have to share, that's all.

So, let us get up and reach out. Let us extend a hand to anyone and everyone who is dead and dying in their secrets, their struggles, their problems, their addictions and their sins. Let us say, "Come with us, we are going to God. We are going to life."

Everyone needs what we have been given.

Keep Making the Choice

"We want to live well, but our foremost efforts should be to help others live well."
      I Corinthians 10:24 *The Message*

"For He claims all, because He is love and must bless. He cannot bless us unless He has us. When we try to keep within us an area that is our own, we try to keep an area of death. Therefore, in love, He claims all. There's no bargaining with Him."
      - C. S. Lewis

Having had a spiritual awakening as the result of these Steps, we tried to carry the message to others, and to practice these principles in all our affairs.

If we ever think that our healing is primarily for our benefit, the selfishness of our thinking reveals just how little we have been healed. On the other hand, when we believe that our healing is to be lived out for the benefit of others, our lives will bear witness to how we have been healed already. In either case, there is just one remaining question and it will never change. We will face it day in and day out, minute by minute, with every breath we take. The question is, who owns us? Will we live for God and others, or will we die in addiction and shame? The answer we give to this question will determine what kind of people we will be and how we will live out our lives.

How we answer this question is not the end of our responsibility; it's just the beginning. All too often, we tend to compartmentalize our lives and judge ourselves wrongly because we use the wrong criteria to evaluate and measure ourselves. We assume that we are doing well because parts of our life are in good order, while we ignore other areas of our life that are all messed up. Or, we judge ourselves too harshly because of one mistake, when in reality there is significant progress that we don't see.

Compartmentalizing and judging ourselves in this way is like determining the winner of a baseball game after just the first or second inning. It's like judging a painting before the artist has completed his work. We need to always remember that God is the only perfect judge. God does not judge us by the pieces or compartments of our lives, and we shouldn't judge ourselves that way either. He recognizes that the whole package of our lives, beginning with the condition of our hearts, is what really counts. He never looks down on us with a red pen and a grade book in hand. He judges us according to the love and righteousness of Christ. So, we should embrace His grace by measuring ourselves by our willingness to follow and obey Him. And even when we fall short and sin, we are not without God's grace. Above all, God wants us to know that we are not worthless or hopeless, even when we are at our worst.

God's grace through Christ gives us the power to recover from our addictions and to walk humbly with God, but it does not make us completely immune to sin or our addictions. We should never think that we are in full control of our lives because, if we go our own way, placing our confidence in ourselves, we become susceptible to relapse and the dire consequences that inevitably follow. If and when we hold even one thing back, we have not really given Him our lives. This doesn't mean that walking with God is an all or nothing thing, because it isn't. Walking with God is progressive. Walking with God is a growth in which we expand and enlarge our acceptance and expression of the grace that He has already given us.

All this is to say that no matter how well or how poorly we have surrendered our lives to God, there is still more to be offered up. Surrender is never relevant in the past tense, but it is always relevant in the here and now. We have to be willing to give the whole of our lives to God, all the good and all the bad, the best that we possibly can, or our life as a whole will not belong to Him at all.

Steve Shares His Life

"Be ready to speak up and tell anyone who asks why you're living the way you are, and always with the utmost courtesy."
I Peter 3:15 *The Message*

"True ambition is the deep desire to live usefully and walk humbly under the grace of God."
- Alcoholics Anonymous

Having had a spiritual awakening as the result of these Steps, we tried to carry the message to others, and to practice these principles in all our affairs.

My family has owned a lumber business for over 80 years. My grandfather started it and my father and his two brothers continued to grow it. Even in childhood, I knew that my dad and mom planned for me to go to college first and then come back and work in the family business.

I was very active in high school, lettering in baseball and football, and I always kept my grades up too. And I did more than my fair share of partying at the same time. My friends and I used to throw really big parties out in the woods and fields around the area, where we would drink beer and smoke marijuana. Actually, I only smoked pot at the time because my granddad and my two uncles had had drinking problems. I never saw my dad drink. He told me that he had a drinking problem at one time, so he stopped. I decided pot would be safer because I didn't want to become an alcoholic like my uncles.

My girlfriend, Mattie, and I met when we were seniors. For me it was lust at first sight. She was smart and beautiful, popular and determined to go to college. Almost immediately we became boyfriend and girlfriend. We were inseparable. Our plan was to get into and out of college as quick as we could, and then get married and start a family. But, something unexpected happened. Mattie called me one afternoon to tell me she was pregnant. She and I were sexual on several occasions, always practicing what we thought was "safe sex." We used a condom each time we had intercourse, but the condom did not prevent her from getting pregnant. Needless to say, our plans for the future changed.

We married the summer after graduation. I went to work driving a truck for the family business, Mattie gave birth to our daughter and we settled into a pretty good life. I worked long hours and made good use of the accelerated opportunities I had in a well-established family business. Our daughter was healthy and joyful, Mattie worked hard to be a great mom, and she attended the local community college part-time as well. I continued to smoke marijuana after work and in the evenings. It took the edge off the day and relaxed me. Mattie had immediately stopped all of her partying when she learned she was pregnant. I think she assumed that I would give pot up too, but she never gave me too much grief about it. Still, I knew she wanted me to stop.

Our daughter was about four when I got pulled over by the highway patrol as I was driving home after work. I was a sales rep for the business by then, and I would smoke a bowl or two of pot several times a day to relax and chill out. I had marijuana in the car and I had smoked some just a few minutes before getting pulled over. Well, you can guess what happened. I was arrested for driving under the influence and for misdemeanor possession of marijuana, and I was sentenced to a drug education and diversion program. The program required that I give regular urine tests to verify that I was no longer smoking marijuana. I wasn't happy about this but I wanted to be a good father, a good husband and a good citizen. So, I gave up pot and soon realized that a few beers in the evening or at lunch did a pretty darn good job of replacing pot. I never smoked marijuana again, but I did pick up a pretty strong habit of relying on alcohol to influence the way I felt. It was not too long before alcohol began to cause problems for me.

Mattie and I had a second child, a boy. When he was about two-and-a-half, I realized that I had gone down the wrong road and become something that I never wanted to be. My two uncles still worked in the family business alongside my dad and me. In fact, as I had matured, I had become the spitting image of one of my uncles. We were the same size and shape, we talked alike and we had the same sense of humor. We also drank the same beer and went through each and every day being just a little drunk. Not too much, but just a little. When I was growing up, I had always felt a sense of loathing towards my uncles because of their drinking. I certainly loved them because they were good-hearted and reliable men, but their drinking made them obnoxious at times and it certainly was not what I wanted to become.

I was shocked the day I realized I had become like my uncle who had the habits I didn't like. I caught a glimpse of him and me in a mirror that day as we were leaving a restaurant. I was shocked to see how much I was like him. Both of us had drinks with our lunch that day, and having seen how much alike we looked in the mirror's reflection, I knew then and there that I had become the alcoholic that I never wanted to become. Instead of returning to work, I went home and told Mattie what happened. She could tell I was in a panicked state. I had been drinking for years by then, and alcohol had become more important to me than I knew. And, at the same time, I was desperately afraid that all of my good intentions and dreams for my family had been damaged beyond repair.

Now Mattie had been going to church ever since our daughter was born. In fact, she and my mom had been attending church together. Mattie suggested that I call a pastor she knew from there. Apparently this guy had some experience in helping people with problems like mine. That evening I found myself sitting in his office, where we chatted. He was very relaxed and confident. He seemed to understand the dire pain and concern I felt, but at the same time he didn't share my panic. He explained to me how addiction is a disease and that my addiction probably didn't start with alcohol, it probably started with the pot that I was smoking back in high school. He suggested that I get some professional help. Two days later I entered into a twenty-eight day detox and treatment program. This program had me going to AA meetings and I was surprised at how normal the AA people seemed to be. Actually, the people at the meetings were pretty cool.

Near the end of my twenty-eight days at the treatment center, I was visited by the same pastor from Mattie's church. He told me about Jesus in a way that was different than how I had heard about Him before. The pastor told me how Jesus makes it possible for me to <u>enjoy</u> a relationship with God, and that a relationship with God was more of a personal interaction, not a religious endeavor. In fact, he said that I didn't have to get religious at all; all I had to do was just be honest and open with God, and Jesus would take care of the rest. I guess I should confess by this time I was intrigued about God because of the great way the people from AA and from Mattie's church would talk about Him. It was like He was their friend and helper, not like the big head-busting punisher I thought Him to be. I was thirty-seven days sober when I prayed to God, thanking Him for Jesus and asking Him to live with me and in me.

I completed the treatment program but I have never completed AA. I still go to meetings. I attend church with Mattie and I've gotten involved in the Restoration program for recovering people like me. On Tuesday evenings I set up chairs, make coffee, shake hands and help with the Twelve Step groups. I've been doing this for quite some time now, and I've grown to love the addicted people who come to visit us. There are several treatment centers around the area who bring their clients to visit us. I can't wait to get there on Tuesdays to see them. I know the pain they feel. I know what it is like to have my ego crushed. When they cry, I cry too. I never promise them that their life will be easy or that it will be the way they want it to be. I just tell them about Jesus. I tell them that God does not hold their sins against them, and that His full love and forgiveness is theirs to have if they will just believe it, ask for it and act on it.

I am turning gray now. My daughter is in college and my son is heading that way. Almost every day I look back and fondly remember the day that I went into treatment. Even then, I sensed that my life was not going to be the same again. I was afraid and yet I was ready, too. I wanted to escape the addictions that had plagued my family and me. But, I never expected what I got. In sharing what God has done for me through AA, recovery and, above all, through Jesus, my life is complete.

As I examine myself further, I want to confess that I have often had the silly belief that I was "the king" of my own world. I don't really know how to explain it anymore than that. Maybe it was because I grew up kind of spoiled, but I always thought that I should be immune to suffering, and that if I felt emotional or physical discomfort in any way, I was being treated unfairly. I bet this is why I learned to prefer being disconnected from life through pot and alcohol instead of facing life head-on. And, I think this is why I spent so much of my life flirting with women in very subtle ways. I never cheated on Mattie and I was never into porn or anything like that. I just had an insatiable need for attention and affirmation, which I would get by being charming to women. Having recognized this, I have admitted it to several of my recovery partners and I am working my Twelve Step program and going to meetings to help me deal with what I now know about myself.

In brief, this is how I see my life. I know that I was born into privilege and that I did not have the wherewithal to appreciate it. I have been loved all along, by my family, by my wife and by my children. Most of all and best of all, I have come to know that God has always loved me and that He has and will always love the whole world too. No one needs to be left out. I know, from my own experience, that God loves people who have addictions. And, on top of it all, I believe that those of us who have addictions and who are in recovery are well suited to take in and give out God's love to all of those around us.

Questions Remain

"Surely you desire truth in the inner parts; you teach me wisdom in the inmost place."

Psalm 51:6 *NLT*

"This inrush of God's Holy Spirit heals us naturally – naturally. But it does far more than that. Indeed, as we pursue the spiritual life we lose sight of the physical benefits in our increasing vision of God Himself. We find after a while that we desire God more for His own sake than for ours."

- Agnes Sanford

Having had a spiritual awakening as the result of these Steps, we tried to carry the message to others, and to practice these principles in all our affairs.

Matching up God's grace with our willingness brings about a life-altering shift to our thinking, to our believing, and to the way that we see ourselves and the world around us. As a result of this shift, we have experienced changes in how we spend our time, our talents and our money. We have also seen changes in the way we eat and the way we work in our careers. Most of all, healthy changes are reflected in our relationships. We have become and continue to become the most blessed of all people. We are free to share God's love with others in whatever ways are appropriate.

And it does not stop there. We are responsible for being good stewards of the life that God is building in us. We need to challenge ourselves by facing some tough questions so that we can keep moving away from our addictions and toward a fuller, more intimate relationship with God.

Here are some of the questions that keep coming back to us again and again…

- What is God saying to me today?
- What are the things that I am powerless over?
- How is my life unmanageable?
- What do I need to admit?
- What actions do I need to take?

In the past, we avoided questions like these. We had been afraid of what the answers might reveal about us. But now, fear no longer has to hold us back. We see how difficult questions like these keep us moving forward to a life that is increasingly more honest and worth living.

And after all, isn't that what we were looking for all along?

About Operation Integrity

Operation Integrity exists to help people recover from addiction, leading to radical life transformation. We accomplish this by writing educational and Christ-centered Twelve Step literature, developing recovery and peer support fellowships, and providing public speaking and counseling services.

Operation Integrity

24040 Camino del Avion
Suite A115
Monarch Beach, CA 92629
1-800-762-0430

www.operationintegrity.org
info@operationintegrity.org

**OPERATION
INTEGRITY**

Read When Lost Men Come Home

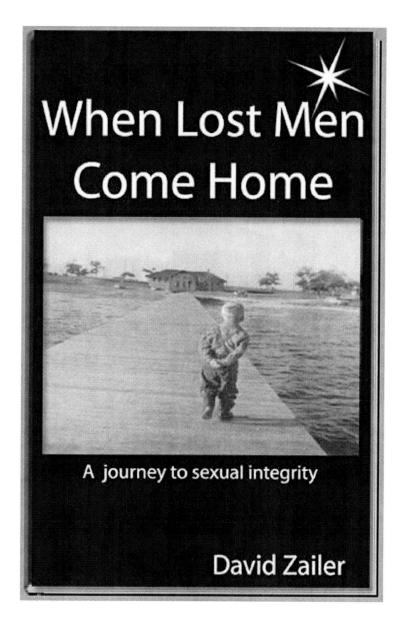

CPSIA information can be obtained at www.ICGtesting.com
Printed in the USA
LVOW091915220312

274295LV00003B/6/P